GOD'S RULES FOR THE GAME OF LIFE

IMPRIMATUR

Having been informed by the Reverend Donald Tracey, who has acted as Censor, that the manuscript, *God's Rules for the Game of Life* has nothing in it contrary to faith and morals and is deserving of a Nihil Obstat, in accordance with the provisions of Canon Law, I grant the necessary Imprimatur to this book.

Given at Lafayette, this, the 20th day of July, 1971.

✝ RAYMOND J. GALLAGHER
Bishop of Lafayette-in-Indiana

Books by Father Leo A. Scheetz, M.A., J.C.B.

GOD AND OURSELVES (3 Volumes)
GOD'S RULES FOR THE GAME OF LIFE
GOING HER WAY
MARY, TREE OF LIFE AND OUR HOPE

GOD'S RULES
FOR THE GAME OF LIFE
How to Get to Heaven

Father Leo A. Scheetz, M.A., J.C.B.

An Exposition–Testament Book

Exposition Press   *New York*

E X P O S I T I O N P R E S S I N C.

50 Jericho Turnpike   Jericho, New York 11753

F I R S T E D I T I O N

LIBRARY OF CONGRESS CATALOG CARD NUMBER: 76-171714

0-682-47346-4

Contents

Preface

This volume contains a skeleton sketch of our Lord's religion. Such has been believed and lived in varying degrees since Jesus ascended into heaven, whence He sent the Holy Spirit upon His Church. It might be truer to say it is a sort of digest of the Catholic Christian religion. The word *Catholic* after almost two thousand years has come to be a dirty word in the vocabulary of many persons. Many there are who would not blush to be called Christian but at the same time would not like to be known as Catholic Christians.

Because of my firsthand information from the many simple Christians that I have received into the Church during the past half century, and their total delight therewith, I find it a labor of love to share with the many the delights that "now are hidden from their eyes."

Not many priests live fifty years in the active priesthood. For my own longevity I am grateful to the dear Lord; and I trust that the contents of this book will continue to bear witness to the beauty of His religion.

L. A. S.

Introduction

Following the Second Vatican Council, much has been attempted in the general catechetical field to relate the teaching of religion to the challenges and responsibilities facing the Church today. As in most such important situations, some have become agitated to a point of making ill-advised suggestions for the reforming and adapting of the basic catechetical material to the new set of circumstances.

Much has been lost in the matter of orthodoxy and stability of faith in people because of the confusion thus produced. Father Leo A. Scheetz in his newest book, *God's Rules for the Game of Life,* makes a serious attempt to preserve the definiteness of the Church's teaching while presenting it in a modern catechetical form. In some of his earlier works, Father Scheetz used the discussion approach as he had developed it with children. In this volume he applies to the adult the system of instruction which he has found profitable and effective through fifty years of his priesthood.

The author conveys the notion that in spite of the fact that conditions change and methods of teaching are advanced, the fundamental teaching of Christ must be preserved and cherished if the continuity of Christ's mission to people is to be assured.

+ RAYMOND J. GALLAGHER
Bishop of Lafayette-in-Indiana

GOD'S RULES FOR THE GAME OF LIFE

CHAPTER 1

The Holy Trinity

FATHER: Your name, please?

BRIGHT: Mr. Bright.

FATHER: What can I do for you?

BRIGHT: I'm interested in religion. That includes the Catholic religion.

FATHER: Who is the girl?

BRIGHT: No girl involved.

FATHER: So your name is Bright? I judge from your appearance that you too are bright, if you will pardon the personal pun.

BRIGHT: I have a sense of humor. Thank you for the compliment.

FATHER: Let me set you at ease at once. I'll be delighted to give you a skeleton course of instructions in our Lord's religion with no obligations on your part. This is my favorite indoor sport. We all boast of our freedom. Let me hasten to tell you there will be nothing to learn by rote. The course will last about six weeks or so. On top of this may I ask you please not to disclose what your religion, if any, may be. The reason I prefer not to know is to avoid seeming ever to be personal to you in any of my remarks.

From the outset I deem it proper to confer upon you the honor of mental integrity and trust you will allow me the same favor.

BRIGHT: Thank you for the compliment. I hasten to reciprocate the favor and to assure you were it otherwise I should not be here.

FATHER: Thank you. I assume that you accept the Bible as an authentic work of history.

BRIGHT: I do, on the basis of Lincoln's alleged slogan, "You can fool all the people some of the time, and some of the people all of the time, but you cannot fool all of the people all of the time." I happen to know that the Bible has withstood the test of time's analysis for two thousand years or more.

FATHER: Our minds with honest thinking plus the Bible will be the only equipment needed in the beginning.

BRIGHT: We are in perfect accord. Let's go.

FATHER: At the outset I should like to ask you a couple of questions for the sake of proper orientation. It matters not to me the nature of your answers. But I do want you to keep in mind the exact answers you give to the following questions.

Number one. At the time of birth into the world, is each and every baby a child of God?

BRIGHT: I would say yes.

FATHER: Number two. Who is or was Jesus Christ?

BRIGHT: I always thought He was God's Son, according to the Bible.

FATHER: Did Jesus have existence before He was born of Mary and called the Son of God?

BRIGHT: No, sir, none whatsoever.

FATHER: Number three. Who was Jesus' father?

BRIGHT: God was His Father, according to the Bible.

FATHER: Would you mind explaining that, please?

BRIGHT: Well, the Bible says Joseph was not His Father even though Joseph was the spouse of Mary, while Mary was the wife of Joseph. I take it that God, who can do all things, created a son or had Mary conceive without the aid of a human sperm as is necessary, according to the laws of nature, regarding every other child born into the world. Here we had an exception to the rule of nature.

FATHER: Why do you think so?

BRIGHT: As I read Luke, God worked this miracle out of deference to Mary and Her promised virginity.

FATHER: Am I to understand you to say that prior to His conception in Mary's womb, Jesus Christ had no existence whatsoever?

BRIGHT: Yes, sir. You understand me correctly.

FATHER: Now, do not fail to keep in your own mind your own answers to the foregoing questions.

1. Your first answer was, "Yes, every child at birth is a child of God."

2. You stated that while Jesus Christ is the Son of God, definitely He had no existence whatever prior to His conception in the womb of His Mother. Might I add, theologians refer to this as the Incarnation. I'll explain that big word later on when the proper time comes.

If someone asked you, Was Jesus a human person? What would be your answer?

BRIGHT: I have never given it much thought, but on the spur of the moment I would have to answer He was a human person. He was a man, according to the Bible.

FATHER: Thank you for your answers. Was He a divine Person?

BRIGHT: No, He was not a divine Person.

FATHER: Do you mind reading from this Protestant Bible? At the start, at least, we shall use the Protestant Bible in order to show you that I am being fair with you who are not a Catholic, Protestant, or non-Catholic.

BRIGHT: What is the difference between a Protestant and a non-Catholic?

FATHER: To me a Protestant is a Christian who claims to be a follower of Christ.

A non-Catholic is one who is neither a Protestant nor

a Catholic. As I said, I do not want to know which you may be. It will not cramp my style in being fair with you. This should inspire a little more confidence.

BRIGHT: You spoke of using the Protestant Bible in preference to the Catholic Bible. Is there any or much difference between them?

FATHER: Yes, there is some difference between them. It depends largely on which edition one uses—aged or of recent vintage. If we use the Protestant edition it will be impossible for you to feel that our instruction has been rigged to suit the case.

I don't mind telling you, according to the experts, that the old-time Protestant edition sacrificed truth somewhat for the sake of style, while the Catholic sacrificed style for the sake of truth.

Today with ecumenism being much alive with the hope of a peaceful, honest union, both have sacrificed truth a little bit in their translations.

BRIGHT: Upon what basis do you make that statement?

FATHER: That statement is predicated on my own translation from the Hebrew and the Greek texts, particularly about some of my pet texts that I have studied over for fifty years. By this I mean, rather than a translation we are given an interpretation.

For an example let us take the familiar text: "Woman, behold, thy son." In the latest version (Protestant) we read in John 19:26: "Mother, behold, your son." While the meaning at this place is not changed, it does not add on the dimension, mentioned in Genesis 3:15, as to whom Moses is referring.

For the present such differences in the Bible will not alter our conclusions.

Please read from John, chapter 1, verse 1. Keep in mind your own answers before now to my questions. Please read.

BRIGHT: I don't seem to find the place.

FATHER: Let me find it for you. Here; now read, please.

BRIGHT: "In the beginning was the Word, and the Word was with God, and the Word was God. The same was in the beginning with God."

FATHER: Hold it, please. Here it is proper to tell you that John wrote in the Greek language the gospel that bears his name.

In the text which you read, the word *was* is used four times. In the Greek language it is called the imperfect tense, or the durative present. Our English language does not have an imperfect tense. This expression, or durative present, is a little bit sharper; it could mean "was" or it could mean "is."

Actually, biblical scholars understand its use here to equate with "timeless existence; relationship to the Father; identity with God." (Cf. *The New American Bible.*)

BRIGHT: What does the term *Word* refer to?

FATHER: As with all primitive peoples, so also in the ancient Near East, the Word is not only the expression of one's thoughts or will but also something concrete that has objective reality, is active, and, as it were, is endowed with the power of the one who speaks it. (That is why in the Semitic languages the term for *word* also means "thing," the object under discussion.) The notions of *thinking* and *speaking* are expressed in the Semitic languages by the same verb; *to think* is to speak in one's heart (Gen. 17:17; 24:45, etc.) and *to speak* is to express, to bring out, what is in one's heart. The spoken word, however, is not merely a sound; it is a real, though invisible thing, just as the breath which at the same time comes out of the mouth. Therefore, *word* (*dabar* in Hebrew) is often parallel with "breath, spirit" (*ruah*).

Once it is spoken it remains in existence and continues

its activity indefinitely: the blessing which Jacob obtained in a deceitful way would not be revoked (Gen. 27:35 ff.).

Word also may mean "power" (*Encyclopedia Dictionary of the Bible*). Combining the two concepts mentioned above, we have: the idea which God has in his heart (mind) from all eternity is the same as God's power. In this way God the Father begets the only substantial Son of the Father. It is an intellectual generation.

Incidentally the very word or name God means "power" in the Bible.

When St. John writes, "The word is with God" and goes on to say that the Word is God, he is informing us that this process of the Word being in the mind or heart of God is the same as God. He confirms it with his very statement "And the Word is God."

This equates with God begetting God. Since God by His very nature is eternal, without beginning, He must be eternally begetting the Word, even as of now. It is an everlasting generation (spiritual) that shall know no end. God, being a spirit, therefore, by the very nature of things can beget but one Son; this, because there is only one God. Hence the Bible calls Him "the only begotten of the Father" when referring to Jesus (John 1:18), the Son of God the Father. Now, read on, please.

BRIGHT: "The same was—is—in the beginning with God." Does this mean the same was—is—a part of God?

FATHER: No. It can't mean that, because there are no parts to God. God is a spirit. It means the whole Word is the whole God, as it says.

BRIGHT: What, then, does it mean?

FATHER: Drop down to 1:14. "And the Word was made flesh [human nature] and dwelt among us" (this is called the Incarnation: coming as present in the flesh, or human nature).

BRIGHT: Then it must mean that the Word who always is (or was) is become the baby Jesus. At the same time it means He is God.

FATHER: Pick up the marbles; you have won.

BRIGHT: Then my answer to your question "Did Jesus have existence before He became man" was a stupendous error!

FATHER: I'm afraid so. This confirms what we said before about the Word.

BRIGHT: When the infant Jesus was conceived in His mother's womb, He became separated from His Father who begot Him. Is this true?

FATHER: No; the only begotten of the Father is not separated from the Father, because John says, "He is with God."

The Father also is present, begetting the Son in his heart, mind, or bosom, as the Bible has it. But not the Father, only God the Son, becomes man as we read in John 1:18. As was stated above, God the Father is always begetting God the Son, which is an intellectual generation that goes on all the time. It shall perdure as long as God is God. That is, forever. The Father and the Son are one God. Jesus said, "I and the Father are one." This means they are one God, who together with the Holy Spirit, as we shall see later, are three Persons in one God.

There is bound to be a union of love between God the Father and God the Son, because both are intelligent. This mutual love of the Father for the Son and of the Son for the Father breathe forth the love in the form of the Third Person, called the Spirit of God. We shall speak of Him later on. John devotes much of his gospel to the Holy Spirit. Read it over when you get home.

These Three Persons are referred to as the Three in One: Three Persons in one and the same nature, which is God.

No one can understand it, but if we study the New

Testament Scripture we come to learn how it does make sense. Each Person operates as a distinct Person. However, each Person always has the one and only nature, which is God. For instance, the Bible says the Father creates through the Son. The Son redeems mankind by His death on the Cross; and the Holy Spirit elevates man to the likeness of God, which is called sanctification.

Continue to read now at John 1:3.

BRIGHT: "All things were made by him; and without him was not any thing made that was made."

FATHER: Turn now to Colossians 1:16 for a verification of this.

BRIGHT: "For by him were all things created, that are in heaven, and that are in earth, visible and invisible, whether they be thrones, or dominations, or principalities, or powers [choirs of angels]: all things were created by him, and for him: and he is before [prior to] all things, and by him all things consist." What does *consist* mean?

FATHER: All things have their beginning and remain created, until man destroys them, by reason of that spoken Word, as we explained already.

BRIGHT: You just mentioned "until destroyed by man." Is man resisting God in this way?

FATHER: No, for the simple reason God created the animal, vegetable, and mineral kingdoms to be of service to man, especially for man's body.

Now turn back to 1:4 and read, please. The Word spoken remains in effect, or active, forever.

BRIGHT: "In him was [is] life; and the life is [was] the light of men. And the light shineth in darkness; and the darkness comprehended it not."

FATHER: The Greek word for "comprehend" or grasp is best understood by the common language of the street, "I will or I won't buy that. In the domain of cats it equates with "to lap up"; or as they say, they did or did not "eat it up."

Further, let me explain "in him was [is] life." That is to say, divine life. If one has within himself this divine life (grace), then that divine life automatically lights up such a person in a divine way.

We understand how the human rational soul lights up our body, to which it is fitted, so that one becomes a human person. Without it one is dead.

If one has within his human soul this divine life (called sanctifying grace), then this divine life automatically lights up such a person so that he is worthy to be called divine.

John informed us they did not accept Him as God, since they put Him to death for saying He was God (John 10:33).

We won't bother with the words in 1:6-9. These you can read privately. Now take number 1:9.

BRIGHT: "That was the true Light, which lighteth every man that cometh into the world. He was in the world, and the world was made by him, but the world knew him not—"

FATHER: Hold it. I forgot to explain above about the "darkness." Natural creation compared to God, who is supernatural, to us is as "darkness." So the world of sin did not comprehend, grasp, or "eat up" what He had to offer. Nor does it today. God is light. The devil is darkness.

Read on.

BRIGHT: "He came unto his own, and his own received him not. But as many as received him, to them he gave the power to become the sons of God, even to them that believe on [in] his name."

FATHER: Hold it. "His own" were the Jewish people of the house of Israel.

BRIGHT: How come in verse 11, He says "they received him not," then here in 12 it says some did receive Him?

FATHER: That is Hebraism. Without saying, in verse 11 there were exceptions, in order to save "paper." John, while he wrote in Greek, still was a Hebrew and full of their eccentricities. Continue.

BRIGHT: "But as many as received him, to them gave he the power to become the sons of God, even to them that believe on [in] his name: which were born, not of blood, nor of the will of the flesh, nor of the will of man, but of God."

FATHER: Here, let me explain. He gave the "power"— meaning what?

Well, immediately before that text you read, "He gave the light." The light was for the mind. Now you read "gave he the power, etc."

Power is in the will. Don't we say in everyday language if one wants to do his thing, willpower is required?

BRIGHT: O.K.

FATHER: That light in the mind when focused on the will warms the will and sets the will power on the man in motion.

Now, I ask you, was your answer to my question correct? When we were children? You answered yes, if you recall.

BRIGHT: Not according to this last text, if I understand it correctly. Would you check me out?

FATHER: Which were born "not of flesh and blood." These words we still use today to mean a human birth. So a *child of God* is not so born at the time of his human birth; "nor of the will of the flesh," which is a human impulse; "nor of the will of man." This is to say that one cannot confer the sonship of God on himself by his own human will. as a large coterie of religionists claim today.

How, then? The record says "but born of God."

In other words, one can't pick himself up by his own

bootstraps and move into heaven, as many erroneously think. We must be born of God, as God's children in good standing, in order to get to heaven.

BRIGHT: How is one born of God?

FATHER: Now turn to John, chapter 3, and read.

BRIGHT: "There was a man of the Pharisees, named Nicodemus, a ruler of the Jews: the same came to Jesus by night, and said unto him, Rabbi, we know that thou art a teacher come from God: for no man can do these miracles that thou doest, except God be with him. Jesus answered and said unto him, "Verily, verily, I say unto thee, except a man be born again he cannot *see* the kingdom of God." Nicodemus saith unto him, "How can a man be born when he is old? Can he enter the second time into his mother's womb, and be born?"

FATHER: Nicodemus' thinking was always on the natural level. He seemed not to understand that Jesus, God, who came from heaven, came to establish a spiritual kingdom on the supernatural level. Many today are of the same cast. They'll find out too late, I'm afraid. These we call materialists, secularists. Sometimes they refer to themselves as existentialists. Jesus then explained in the next words:

"Jesus answered, verily, verily I say unto thee, Except a man [Greek *tis,* one] be born of water and of the Spirit, he cannot *enter* into the kingdom of God. That which is born of the flesh is flesh; and that which is born of the Spirit is spirit. Marvel not that I said unto thee, Ye must be born again."

BRIGHT: Will you explain this somewhat?

FATHER: Delighted!

In the first place let me give you a little of the background.

Nicodemus was a naturally good man but ignorant about spiritual matters. He was a politician. The record says he belonged to the Pharisees and was a ruler of the Jews. That, plus the words you read, shows he was a politician, a backslapper. He would not have been an elected ruler.

The Pharisees were one of two major parties among the Jews: Pharisees and Sadducees. All others, as Herodians, Essenes, etc., were splinter parties. Each party had its own private beliefs, as today.

Nicodemus had listened to Jesus expound publicly about the kingdom of God and the necessity of taking up membership therein. He played both ends of the game. He "came by night," which tells us he did not want to be caught by the party of the Pharisees, in which he was a big wheel. At the same time if the kingdom of God was to become a necessary reality he wanted to get in on the ground floor.

If you noted what you read, it says, "Jesus answered." But it does not inform us what the question was that Jesus answered.

Since "paper" was scarce and expensive, if one was alert he should have guessed what the question might have been.

Nicodemus must have asked, "How does one get to be a member in your so-called kingdom of God?"

Jesus told him "one must be born again." How to become a member seemed not to register with Nicodemus. He must have said: "I can't see it."

Thereupon Jesus replied under oath, of course you can't see it. "Verily, verily, I say unto you unless one is born again he *cannot see* the kingdom of God."

BRIGHT: Where do you find an oath in that text? The Greek has, "Amen, amen, I say unto you, etc."

FATHER: The Protestant text translates by the words "Verily, verily," but this does not capture the nuance or shade of meaning equivalent to an oath.

You see, the Jewish people were prudes in those days. They would not use the word "God" in swearing, so they coined the word *amen,* which the Protestants translate by "verily." Use your own judgment as to which is the stronger word, *amen* or *verily.* The Latin retained amen also.

When Nicodemus missed the boat about being born again, Jesus went still further and told how one is to be reborn in order to *enter* the kingdom of God. Jesus said that except a man (*tis: anyone*) be born of water and of the Spirit, he cannot *enter* the kingdom of God. This rebirth, therefore, is not in apposition with one's present-day birth as is. It is in apposition with the birth the way it was intended by God from the very begining of time to have been.

BRIGHT: Do you mean from the beginning as referring to Adam and Eve?

FATHER: You are hot. Yes, indeed.

BRIGHT: Why is not one a child of God when he is born of his own mother?

FATHER: Here is where original sin enters the picture. Many religionists do not believe in original sin.

BRIGHT: Why not?

FATHER: It sometimes is difficult to explain or account for the vagaries of other persons' minds. Most Protestant Christians hold that it is faith that one has in his heart that makes him a member of the Church. They say Baptism as explained is a superstition. How, say they, can a dab of water and a few words put God in the soul?

BRIGHT: Did they believe in original sin in the Old Testament?

FATHER: They surely did. Listen to David: "In [the state of] sin did my mother conceive me" (Psalm 50:7).

Yes, I know, I added the words "the state of" so as to keep David's words honest. Most people read that text and conclude that the Psalmist is talking about sex. From this they jump to the erroneous conclusion that parental mating or union is a sin. The author of the Psalms was merely using a figure of speech for the sake of saving expensive "paper" and leaving it to the official reader to explain.

Jesus wants us to believe in original sin according to the last texts (John 3:1 ff.).

BRIGHT: What was the original sin?

FATHER: That's a good question. It had its origin with Adam and Eve. When God created our first parents, originally it was His plan that Parent and his wife should retain the likeness of God that God put in them, as we read in Genesis 5:1: "In the day that God created man, in the likeness of God made He him . . . and called their name man."

It is interesting to note the vocabulary used by Moses versus that of John. Moses speaks of the likeness of God in Parent. John refers to Him as "Light" versus "darkness": the Light who came to replace that likeness of God that was lost to mankind by Parent.

BRIGHT: Does this mean that God created them after His own likeness, namely God-like?

FATHER: Yes, sir. You have it. Or to turn it around, unless one is divine (God-like) he is not human. God first created them and then moved into their hearts or souls so they were made like Him.

BRIGHT: How did they lose that likeness?

FATHER: By not obeying the rules for the game of life. They believed Serpent rather than God. They were created with free will. Serpent said to them, "For God does know that in the day ye eat thereof, then your eyes shall be opened, and ye shall be as gods, knowing good and evil." When Serpent said, "Your eyes shall be opened," he was referring to the exercise of free will. And when Serpent said, "Ye shall be as gods," he was referring to himself and his ilk who had had their eyes opened to their eternal despair.

They became false gods as soon as they lost God's likeness. The entire story about the Fall of Adam and Eve, if read in the Hebrew language, seems to find itself repeated today by countless numbers who say, "I don't believe in this religion stuff." Like Nicodemus they say, "I can't see it." And indeed they don't. Can the blind see? These persons are blind for want of the organs of sight: faith, which comes with Baptism, but which they call superstition.

Later on I will ask you to read about the fall or sin of the heavenly spirits. One of them, Michael by name, said to Lucifer, "Who is like God?" This tells us that Lucifer in his arrogance and pride would not serve God-made-man but would be his own god. It was then that Lucifer and his followers lost the likeness of God which is necessary to be admitted into heaven.

That little phrase "Who is like God?" spells out in concentrated form the one word Michael in the Hebrew (Mi-cha-el).

CHAPTER 2

The Kingdom of Heaven

This whole story in Genesis in the first few chapters is a play on words, written in an obscure manner to disallow the pagans in Egypt and elsewhere from ridiculing the sacred truth.

BRIGHT: What is the tree of good and evil?

FATHER: It must be the tree of the human soul with its mind and will rooted in the soil (dust) of the human body. The word *adam* is a Hebrew word meaning "red dust."

BRIGHT: Then man is not really free if he can't do what he pleases?

FATHER: There are two kinds of freedom: functional or physical freedom to do as one pleases and moral freedom, which is the freedom to do as one ought to do. "The truth shall make you free" (John 8:32), said Jesus when on earth. That is to say, we are only free to do the right thing. But we are free to choose how this may be done. But to do the wrong thing is not freedom. It is slavery. Look up St. Paul right quick, Romans 6:16: "Know ye not, that to whom ye yield yourselves servants to obey, his servants ye are to whom ye obey; whether of sin unto death, or of obedience unto righteousness?"

BRIGHT: In reality, then, we do not have too much freedom, according to those texts.

FATHER: If one has an erroneous notion of what true liberty is, then you are quite correct. Look up II Corinthians 3:17: "Where the Spirit of the Lord is, there is liberty." Continuing, Paul says, "Stand fast therefore in the liberty wherewith Christ hath made us free, and be not entangled with the yoke of bondage" (Gal. 4:1). The word *death* used above in Romans 6:16 is death to the likeness of God to the soul; or mortal sin.

BRIGHT: It seems we think of freedom from, more than freedom to do?

FATHER: Freedom from authority and free to do as God, who is Supreme Truth, orders, yes.

BRIGHT: Where does the devil come into the picture?

FATHER: There is a story about him in the Book of Revelation (Apocalypse) 12:1 ff. and in Isaias 14:11-15, and otherwise scattered throughout the whole Bible. You can read those parts at home and save a little time. If you have some questions, I'll answer them at the next class.

BRIGHT: What was it that caused Satan to abuse his free will?

FATHER: It is scattered throughout the Bible that God created the spirits, erroneously referred to as angels, before He created man. God gave them their trial. God apprised them of the fact the He would come into the world some day as the Son of God made man; and to be worshipped as king in both His divine and His human nature.

This is to say that all of these spirits would have to adore Him as man in His human nature; together with the proper honor owed to His own Mother: He as King and She as Queen Mother.

Lucifer—meaning "bearer of light"—was highest of those rebelling. He said, "I'll be damned if I am going to worship a man." Men are lower than are spirits, thought he in his pride. But Lucifer was in error. Without saying as much, God implied that the Word of God, or God the Son, was (is) a divine person from all eternity. He was already then in existence as God but not a man until He would be born as man.

We do know a person acts with and through his nature. The Bible speaks of the Father who has certain chores which He did and still does; the same with God the Son, and the same with God the Holy Spirit. It would be nonsense to speak of three Gods. The conclusion must be there are three Persons with the same God nature. What one Person does the other two also do because all three are one God.

From all that has been said it is evident that God the Son, become man, is not a human person. He does have a human nature, without being a human person.

BRIGHT: Why?

FATHER: One person cannot be two persons at the same time. Since the Son of God is a divine Person from all eternity and is constantly being begotten of the Father as we learned it, He cannot stop being a divine Person in order to be some human person.

This divine Person with His human nature is entitled to be worshipped as God. Lucifer thought otherwise. He decided, he, Lucifer, was more than Jesus and should be accorded honor in keeping therewith. He said, "I will not serve" (Jer. 2:20).

Paul knocks this false idea of Satan's into a cocked hat when he says, "For unto which of the angels said he at any time, "Thou art my Son, this day have I begotten thee? And again, I will be to Him a Father, and He shall be to me a Son?" (Heb. 1:5). You might at your leisure read the other texts preceding that one.

Continuing, Paul says, "And again when he bringeth in the first-begotten into the world, he saith, And let all the angels of God worship him" (Heb. 1:6).

BRIGHT: What did you mean a moment ago when you said "spirits, sometimes erroneously called angels"?

FATHER: Only a few times did God use certain spirits to bring messages to earth. That is what the word angel means, namely, a messenger. The archangel Gabriel did a messenger's job for God, as we shall soon see. So did Michael, as you read in Revelation 12:1 ff.

So did Raphael, as one can find out by reading the Book of Tobias. (It's a good story; read it sometime.)

BRIGHT: Why are these messengers called angels pictured with wings?

FATHER: It is difficult to put an abstract idea in picture form. A picture is worth a thousand words was known long before *Life* magazine opted for their use. A spirit moves quick as thought. Way back when, the fastest-moving thing on earth was a bird, with wings.

Time was when a messenger in our day might have been pictured as a Western Union boy with a bicycle and his basket. This would not have been a symbol of speed.

BRIGHT: You asked me a couple questions. Am I privileged to ask a question here?

FATHER: By all means; ask lots of them. You know, a good teacher anticipates the questions. If not, then ask.

BRIGHT: I would not like you to think me an atheist. But I would like to know how you would go about proving the existence of God.

FATHER: In the first place no one can *prove* that there is a God. Nor can one *prove* there is no God.

Secondly, that's for the birds. Theoretically, someone might insist he is an atheist, but practically speaking I don't admit there is such a person as an atheist.

By the mere fact that someone denies the existence of God he is admitting there is a God. Why? To deny the existence of God is the same as taking God away. But if you took Him away, then He must have existed before you took him away (mentally, of course). If He existed, then He still exists, because God *is*. Period. That's His nature, or He would not be God.

His existence might be demonstrated, but not proven. Even your own existence cannot be proven. It can be demonstrated.

BRIGHT: How?

FATHER: Give me a shingle. Stand up.

BRIGHT: Ouch!

FATHER: OK. Satisfied? Sometime read Psalm 13. It appears the Psalmist agrees with this. On the practical level there is no such thing as an atheist. The Psalmist says, "The fool says in his *heart* there is no God."

The word *fool* in Greek is our English word *moron*. A moron is someone with about 51 per cent normal intelligence. Even a moron does not say so in his mind, he says it with his heart, or bad will. He does not want to entertain the thought that there is a God, so he develops a bad will.

You might be interested in this human-interest story. One day as chaplain of a hospital I was making the daily rounds. I came upon a new patient, in no pain or misery whatsoever. "Can I help you?" "No, no," he boasted, "I'm an atheist." "So you impolitely are telling me that I am a fraud?" "Oh, no, I don't mean it that way." "Let me tell you something, young man. Whenever you get a real good bellyache, or when the thunder and lightning is crashing round your ears, or your bed starts heaving during an earthquake, believe you me you will start saying your prayers."

He replied, "I might say, 'O God—if there is a God—have mercy on my soul—if I have a soul.' "

Does that last sentence not sound like a moron speaking? All the while he is admitting there is a God.

Suffice it to say any normal person—child or adult—

instinctively realizes the existence of God. This, for the simple reason that the Creator left the very imprint of His existence to such an extent that there is a saying among men, "The very existence of God is co-natural to us. It is part of our very nature."

BRIGHT: How can one be sure that all of the things you tell me are believable?

FATHER: We are getting on pretty fast. That is a good question. Let me pause here to explain something you never thought of—a thing I'm sure you will accept.

If you recall, at the outset I referred to the Bible as a reliable work of history. You so agreed, as I recall it.

From this reliable work of history it is absolutely necessary that we prove that the Bible is also a religious book. To do this we must first find out in this history book how to arrive at that knowledge, namely, that the Bible is also a religious book, or a book on religion, and what the phase of religion contained in it means.

Here is the way we will go about it. We discovered from John that *the* Word is an idea from God's mind. *A* word is an idea from anyone's mind or heart.

We learned that *the* Word is the most important idea from the mind or heart of God. In fact, *the* Word is God as we read it.

This being the case, it well behooves us to sit up and take notice of everything He said or did while upon earth.

Since He is God who speaks, and God who acts, we must search Bible history for everything He said and did.

Among the many things He did, the very first was to gather around Him disciples (learners). He conducted a school for them up in the mountain quiet. He preached about many things. The main issue was the gospel of the kingdom (Matt. 4:23). Nicodemus got interested, remember?

There are over two hundred references to His "kingdom" in the New Testament. After some schooling among the disciples He selected twelve men whom He called Apostles, because they were *sent* officially by Jesus to preach the gospel of the kingdom all over the world, but never to preach their own opinions.

When He was getting things organized, He asked the Twelve one day this question: "Who do people say that the Son of [the] Man is?" They replied, "Some say John the Baptist, others Elijah, still others Jeremiah or one of the prophets." "And you, ——, who do you say that I am?" "You are the Messiah," Simon Peter answered, "the Son of the living God." Jesus replied, "Blessed are you, Simon son of John! Flesh and blood has not revealed this to you, but my Father who is in heaven, he has revealed it to you." "And I say also unto thee, That thou art Peter [Rock: *Cephas*], and upon this rock I will build my church [assembly: *ekklesia*]; and the gates of hell [the devil] shall not prevail against it. And I will give unto thee the keys of the kingdom of heaven: and whatsoever thou shalt bind on earth shall be bound in heaven; and whatsoever thou shalt loose on earth shall be loosed in heaven. Then he charged His disciples that they should tell no man that he was Jesus the Christ." (Matt. 16:13 ff.).

BRIGHT: Why does one place use the expression "kingdom of God" and in other places we read "kingdom of heaven?"

FATHER: Good boy! I told you you looked bright. I love questions.

It has already been mentioned that the Jews were prudes. Since Matthew wrote his gospel to the Jews in Palestine solely, he had to use the expression "kingdom of heaven." But the other writers who wrote to people whom civilization of that day had caught up with, they were able to use the latter expression like they thought, namely, kingdom of God. Or should we say, they became more sophisticated by the time John wrote some forty years later, more or less!

BRIGHT: Is one to conclude that since Jesus promised to give the "keys" to Simon Peter, there is to be found therein the same symbol as when the keys to a city are conferred today, say on astronauts?

FATHER: Good boy again, only with this difference: Today a presentation of the keys is an honorary gesture; in Jesus' words, He was talking turkey. How do we know this? From the rest of the words used on the same occasion.

Jesus was using the language of a parliamentarian making laws, also promising Simon the office of president of His kingdom at some future date.

In fact, Jesus was telling Simon that some day he would become Jesus' own successor. The Bible is full of expressions referring to Christ as the "Rock." It was for the reason that Simon was to become successor to Christ, the Rock, that Jesus called Simon "rock," meaning infallible or immovable in matters pertaining to the Lord's teachings, if and whenever Simon Peter should so declare himself on some given occasion that involved Jesus' teachings. We shall see more of this in a later section.

CHAPTER 3

Infallibility—The First Pope

In the last lesson reference was made to Christ in no uncertain terms. Jesus makes it plain that the "rock" (Peter: Cephas) is to be successor to "the Rock," namely Christ, at some future date. He does not as yet say when.

In John 21:15-18 we find the promise fulfilled not till after His Resurrection in these words: "Jesus saith to Simon Peter, Simon, son of Jonas,* lovest thou me more than these? He saith unto him, Yea, Lord; thou knowest that I love thee. He saith unto him, Feed my lambs. He saith unto him again the second time, Simon, son of Jonas, lovest thou me? He saith unto him, Yea, Lord; thou knowest that I love thee. He saith unto him, Feed my sheep. He saith unto him the third time, Simon, son of Jonas, lovest thou me? Peter was grieved because he said unto him the third time, Lovest thou me? And he said unto him, Lord, thou knowest all things; thou knowest that I love thee. Jesus saith unto him, Feed my sheep."

BRIGHT: Is there any significance in the fact that Jesus asked Simon Peter three times whether or not he loved Him?

FATHER: Some think it was because Simon Peter denied Jesus three times before the woman. It is an educated guess. Maybe it is so, maybe not. It is a pious thought, however.

BRIGHT: Who are the lambs and who are the sheep?

FATHER: The lambs are the disciples, and the sheep are the Apostles. The lambs are the successors to the disciples

---

*Jonas in Hebrew means John in English.

who are the people and the clergy—the learners. The sheep are the Apostles and their successors, the bishops, who together with Peter are the official teachers. Peter is to keep everybody honest.

BRIGHT: Honest on what?

FATHER: Honest on His truths, if any get lost or have any doubts. Honest on how to get to heaven. If you turn to John, chapter ten, you'll find our Lord compares this kingdom to a sheepfold where the sheep go in and out to pasture to be fed. He calls Himself the "good shepherd," but He refers also simply to "another shepherd" who leads the sheep out to pasture, to and fro (John 10:2).

Further, Jesus says "I am the *door* of the sheepfold through me the sheep enter, etc."

Again, Jesus implies that the sheepfold is locked because some thieves and robbers go in through another way than the door which He is.

We read that about a year before His death He promised Simon, son of Jonas, the keys and authority. If we read carefully we shall discover that Peter is to be the spoken "voice" of the silent Christ in the years to come, after His Ascension (John 10:17, 27).

If not Peter, then his successor, because His kingdom is to last till the end of the world; but anyone knows that Peter or no one else is to last that long.

Jesus will always be speaking through the *voice* of "Peter" or his successor. This is clear because Jesus says in John 10:27, "They shall hear my *voice* and they shall follow me." Do you wish to look it up?

BRIGHT: No, I'll take your word for it. You have proved right along you know what you are talking about.

FATHER: Thank you! Let us return to that last text about the "voice." Jesus did not say, "They shall hear my voice and they shall follow my voice." He said, "They shall

hear my voice and they shall follow *me*." That is a whale
of a difference. Jesus about to ascend into heaven leaves
Peter commissioned to be his own voice.

BRIGHT: What does *Pope* mean?

FATHER: It is a corruption of the Greek word *pappa*—papa
in English—meaning "head." Christ is head of His kingdom. The Pope, his successor, or Vicar, is also the head,
or *pappa*, Pope. Rock for Rock: immovable or fixed. He
will not falter.

BRIGHT: Is the kingdom of God or heaven coextensive with
the Church or vice versa?

FATHER: This is hard to answer. I suppose to say it correctly
one should answer, in some ways yes, in other ways no.

For example, is an unborn child a full member of the
human race? The answer: in some ways yes, in some ways
no.

I think all will agree that while an unborn child does
have certain rights, it does not have the full rights or stature
the same as a child that is born.

Would you say that our Lord answered your question
when He said to Nicodemus, "Unless one is born again he
cannot [not *will not*] *see* the kingdom of God" but it takes
water and the Holy Spirit in order that one may *enter* the
kingdom of God?

Jesus spoke of "other *sheep* I have that are not of this
fold, then too must I bring and there shall be one fold
and one shepherd." Perhaps this could be the answer to
your question.

If one reads the Scripture carefully, there is one fold
and one shepherd from the start. There still is. It shall not
be entirely one till the end of time. This means when all
get to heaven, those who so will it.

BRIGHT: I looked up the story of Tobias but found it among
the Apocrypha. What does that word mean?

FATHER: It means the books that are held to be doubtful as not being worthy of being classified in the canon of Sacred Scripture. Perhaps spurious is a better word. The Protestants reject them as canonical because the Jews do not accept them.

BRIGHT: Why do the Catholics accept them?

FATHER: 1. Because they are found in the Septuagint version, which was translated from Hebrew into Greek for the Jews in distant lands (Egypt) that had forgotten their Hebrew.

2. When Jesus was on earth He quoted from them as reliable Scripture, "as is written."

3. Our infallible authority puts her OK on them.

They were written in Greek, a foreign tongue, and for this reason the old-time Jew would not accept them. Nothing good, said they, would come from a foreigner. Personally, I think the real reason was that they proved that the Logos, the Word, is the true Messiah.

BRIGHT: We got past a question I had quite some time ago. I wanted to ask if that water and the Holy Spirit is what is today called Baptism?

FATHER: What Jesus refers to as water and the spirit—yes, that is actual Baptism, which is the right of initiation into the kingdom or for membership in the Church, which is absolutely necessary for all men born of Adam. When Jesus spoke about being born again in order to *see* the kingdom of God, He was referring to what St. Augustine called invisible Baptism.

BRIGHT: What is that?

FATHER: That is the love of God which makes contact with God sufficiently so that one may desire the kingdom of God as one sees it. A Baptism of desire.

To desire Baptism is one thing, and to have the Baptism of desire is something else, or the invisible Baptism.

BRIGHT: You mentioned before that the sheep and the lambs are a symbol of all members in the Church—laity, people, clergy, and bishops. How do you know that?

FATHER: Let me quote to you from Paul, about the wisest of all the apostles, who himself was an apostle because he was sent in a unique way to bear witness to the gospel, or to teach. Listen to what he said: "For though ye have ten thousand instructors in Christ, yet have not many fathers: for in Christ Jesus I have *begotten* you through the gospel" (I Cor. 4:15).

Paul, according to that text, was the "sheep" who sired the lambs (Corinthians) by cross-fertilization of the word of God with the grace of God.

BRIGHT: What do you mean by the grace of God?

FATHER: Back in John 1 we read about the Word (Son of God) enlightening every man that comes into the world. That "light" is called grace. While it illumines the mind, at the same time it is for free, or gratis. Hence grace.

BRIGHT: We also read, to as many as received Him to them He gave the power to become the sons of God. Is that grace too?

FATHER: Excellent thinking. The impulse that God puts in the will to follow God while leaving the man free to go the wrong way if he chooses is indeed the grace of God. That too comes for free, which is God's grace.

BRIGHT: The expression "that believe in, or on, his name." What does that mean?

FATHER: That is a standardized expression; or perhaps it could be called an idiom, which means that anything Jesus said or did has His name on it. He stands back of it, guarantees it. General Motors stands behind any product with its name on it.

BRIGHT: I think we are or were on the question of credibility.

FATHER: Quite so. Is it beginning to dawn upon you that Jesus organized His Church in a truly legal manner with the power (authority) to make laws and to rescind ("loose") them? Does it begin to appear that if Peter (Rock), or the Pope, is successor to the chief Rock, Jesus, Jesus gave him all power which He had? That is to say, He made Peter infallible. This means that when Peter or his successor feeds either the lambs or the sheep the truths of Jesus there can be no error.

Before we get too far afield let us return to our original subject. We have been trying to establish the faultless logic of considering the Bible a religious book.

First we established from history (Bible and otherwise) that Christ did establish a sane and sound organization with parliamentary procedure and perfect authority from Him.

Secondly that sound, and sane, and divine, and authoritative kingdom, or Church, is empowered solely to teach Christ's teachings, which He brought from heaven, as well as to interpret them.

It is also clear that the Bible is the book on religion, together with tradition, that contains as well as guarantees the truths or revelations of God which Christ brought from heaven as the rules whereby men must live and get to heaven.

BRIGHT: Sounds logical, but is this to say that the Pope cannot commit a sin? What is the big word for that called?

FATHER: *Impeccable* is the word you are after. No, indeed, there is no such promise as that. The Pope has to earn his way to heaven the same as the rest of us by following the rules for the game of life.

BRIGHT: When Peter died, didn't infallibility die with him?

FATHER: Lots of people feel that way. If they thought for a minute, they would know better. Why?

1. Christ said His kingdom would last till the end of the world.

2. Jesus said, "The gates of hell [devils] will not prevail against [overcome] my kingdom." The devil is having a field day today, but he shan't prevail.

3. That being the case, infallibility must perdure until the end of time.

4. Infallibility is not a charism, as many say it today. It is not a personal gift, which a charism is. Were it a personal gift it would have died with the first Pope.

5. It is an official gift to be used by the Pope for the welfare of all members, as we said before. It is not a personal gift or attribute.

6. Infallibility is attached to the office. It comes with the office of Pope.

7. If the Pope resigned he would not resign infallibility in some special ceremony. That would be silly. If he resigned his office, then infallibility would remain attached to the office for his successor at the time of his successor's election with which to be endowed.

You asked a moment ago if the Pope is impeccable. He probably wishes he were. So do I wish I were impeccable. Quite the contrary. Jesus said to Simon Peter one day, "And you, Peter, being converted, confirm your brothers."

BRIGHT: Why, then, address the Pope as Your Holiness if he is not impeccable?

FATHER: Oh, the tyranny of words! That expression merely informs us that the Pope is the spokesman, the Vicar of Christ, *who is Holiness but not the Pope.*

BRIGHT: I've been digesting these things. It seems to me you have made a pretty neat argument in favor of the credibility of the Church for which you are the spokesman.

FATHER: There are several texts which repeat this thought among the gospel reporters. How about this one from Luke 10:16: "He that heareth you heareth me; and he that despiseth you despiseth me and him that sent me"?

BRIGHT: You mentioned that Peter the Pope or his successors were to feed the Apostles (sheep) or bishops and keep them straight about Jesus' teachings. Is there any example in the Bible where this happened?

FATHER: Yes, indeed. If you turn to the Acts of the Apostles (chap. 15) written by Luke, who is alleged to have been Paul's secretary, you will find an example: "And the apostles and elders [priests; presbyters] came together to consider of this matter." The point of discussion was whether circumcision had any place in Jesus' New Testament religion. After most everyone had had his say, or, as the record reads, "when there had been much disputing, Peter rose up, and said unto them, Men and brethren, ye know that a good while ago [about 14 years] God made choice among us, that the Gentiles by mouth [voice] should hear the word of the gospel [good news], and believe, etc., etc."

Peter here is giving an infallible decision on feeding the Apostles, etc., including the learned St. Paul. Peter acted as the official spokesman or voice of the Word.

Observe how Peter presented his portfolio of credentials to all present. How God made choice among us, etc., etc. (Acts 15:7).

BRIGHT: How did God make the choice?

FATHER: They were present when Jesus promised the keys (authority) and also when He conferred it. ("Feed my sheep, etc.")

BRIGHT: Is this to be compared to the hassle the Catholic bishops of the world, etc., had at Vatican II?

FATHER: Precisely. If you followed it, there was quite a heated debate concerning the Blessed Mother. When put to a vote, that vote came off very close.

Later on, Pope Paul VI added on his own: "Mary is the Mother of the Church." As a matter of fact, whatever the bishops voted on had no force unless and until the Pope had OK'd any or all of the points discussed. He has the power of veto if He decides it necessary or useful.

BRIGHT: Well, then, of what value is the Council if all the bishops together can't give a lasting decision without the Pope?

FATHER: Always remember truth cannot be decided by a vote. Example: One day a strange-looking bird got into a classroom. There was considerable discussion among the high-schoolers whether it was a male or a female bird. Finally some girl said, "Let us take a vote on it." A vote would not have solved the problem. The most a vote could do would be to decide how many were right in their view, and how many were wrong, once the truth was finally established.

BRIGHT: Do I understand properly that the Pope cannot make a mistake?

FATHER: In matters left by our Lord in what is called the Deposit of Faith, you are correct.

BRIGHT: How about questions of science?

FATHER: Such matters per se have nothing to do with getting to heaven. All that Jesus brought from His Heavenly Father concerning the requirements for the rules for the game of life He left with the Church in what history records as His revelations, which are to be found in the Deposit of Faith.

BRIGHT: The Pope, then, cannot put forth his own ideas for the faithful?

FATHER: No. The revelations that our Lord brought from

heaven closed with the death of the last Apostle. Nothing new or different has ever been added since. The Pope, be it said in passing, must first believe whatever he teaches us to believe as coming from Christ. He cannot prescribe on his own.

When Jesus was on earth, He was wont to say, "My doctrine is not mine but his who sent me" (John 7:16).

Even Jesus did not reveal anything on His own authority.

BRIGHT: If Jesus was sent to teach, does that make Him a missionary?

FATHER: Good thinking. Now you see why a while back I insisted that we must believe that Jesus is God and is one with the Father and the Holy Spirit.

When you say you believe something, anything, about religion, what do you mean by that word?

BRIGHT: It is what I think, or it is my studied opinion from reading the Bible. What does the word *believe* mean to you?

FATHER: It means I accept any and everything the Church believes and teaches without the slightest shadow of a doubt. It is an assent of my mind to all that is proposed for my belief by Christ and His Church.

When the Church has spoken, there remains no place for any previously studied opinion. Example: There are three Persons in one God. The second Person became man, and Mary is His Mother.

This faith is created at the time of Baptism as a new organ of sight. It is often referred to as the "eyes of faith," and as St. Paul says, "it does not disappoint" (Rom. 10:11). St. Peter, the first Pope, said the same thing. Read St. Peter's first letter (2:1-10).

All that is in the Bible is classified as divine faith. And any of the truths of the Bible or tradition proposed for our belief are called divine Catholic faith.

Someone may reject an idea in the Bible because he fears it is not properly reported. He could not be censured for that. But once the Church has spoken with finality, then we must say, "I believe."

BRIGHT: What's to keep the Pope from erring?

FATHER: God will do that. He said, "The gates of hell [the devil] shall not prevail against my church." How God will do that, He never said. However, we dare not doubt God's word to that effect.

BRIGHT: Can't one believe whatever he pleases? We are free.

FATHER: As stated already, one is functionally free to believe anything one pleases, but no one is morally free except to believe only God's truth that proceeds from the mouth of the Father once it has so been declared by the Pope, His Vicar.

BRIGHT: How can the Pope know what came from the mouth of the Father?

FATHER: Put it this way. The mind of the Pope is so in harmony with the mind of God that the two minds are as one. God's mind is in the Bible and also in tradition.

You won't say that the mind of God can err, will you? Either the written or the spoken word proceeds from God.

BRIGHT: No, I know better than to think or say that.

FATHER: OK. Then if God's mind and the Pope's mind are as one mind, how can the Pope err in matters of religion!

BRIGHT: Yes, but I read where Popes have made mistakes over the years. Does this not give the lie to papal infallibility?

FATHER: You never read where any Pope erred regarding any doctrine contained in the Deposit of Faith.

BRIGHT: How about Galileo and the Inquisition?

FATHER: Those matters were never contained in the Deposit of Faith, albeit they did brush against religious practice because of imprudence. We dare not compare standards of bygone years with the standards of today.

BRIGHT: From what you have said concerning the bishops, all assembled at a Council, their word does not count for too much if the Pope can veto it.

FATHER: You may put it that way if you so desire. However, keep in mind that the Pope can learn much from the bishops assembled, whether it be practical or not to define such or such as a truth contained in the Deposit of Faith.

The bishops assembled may consider "such" to be of an impractical nature, at the present time according to the nature of the people in their respective territories.

Such a reaction occurred at the time Pius IX wanted to define, and did so define, the infallibility of the Pope in Vatican I.

Some few objected. He did it anyway. Even our Lord when on earth said, "Many other things I have to say to you, but you cannot bear them now."

Might we say more on this question the next class!

Some are still beefing about the wisdom of defining infallibility after over one hundred years.

BRIGHT: Where do you stand on the matter?

FATHER: It was a wise move. It may have lost some to the Church (old Catholics and today's existentialists), but infallibility has given peace of mind to all the rest of us.

CHAPTER 4

Deposit of Faith—Original Sin

BRIGHT: It seems to me the Pope controlled Vatican II as to the agenda which was to be discussed.

FATHER: That's the part of wisdom. Why allow the bishops to discuss some point that our Lord settled already when on earth!

BRIGHT: Just why so much concern about papal infallibility?

FATHER: It is concerned with the rules for the game of life and how to get to heaven. Listen to these words of Jesus: "All power [authority] is given unto me in heaven and in earth. Go ye therefore, and make disciples of all nations, baptizing them in the name of the Father, and of the Son, and of the Holy Spirit, teaching them to observe all things whatsoever I have commanded you; and, lo, I am with you alway, even unto the end of the world. Amen. (Matt. 28:18.)

In Mark 16:16 we read: "Go ye into all the world and preach the gospel to every creature. He that believeth and is baptized shall be saved; but he that believeth not shall be damned."

In some respects infallibility is the great plank on which we stand. It safeguards or guarantees the safety of our faith. It closes the gap of credibility.

BRIGHT: Those are pretty potent words. They sound as if Jesus meant business.

FATHER: You want to know something? In the U.S.A. the only games that are played strictly according to the rules are athletic games. Sometimes these fail. The game of life is played according to various opinions. We have precious little government out of Washington. Instead, almost every interest has its own rules, such as unions for labor, unions for almost everything.

BRIGHT: Why did Jesus pass the power, or authority, he had from His Father over to the Church?

FATHER: If you recall, the human family originally in the beginning was presided over by Parent. But he flunked out. The way he would go was the way the human family after him would go.

It appears that Serpent sold Eve a bill of goods not to bother about religion. She ate it up, and so did Parent: not to follow God's rules. At that, God promised a Redeemer who would come into the world. He would take over the human family in person and lead them back to God, as many as there should be who were interested in becoming members of His family and observing the rules of the game.

We read in Genesis 3:15 these words: "I will put enmity between you and the woman, and between your seed [offspring] and her seed; he shall crush your head [authority], and you shall lie in wait for her heel."

BRIGHT: Who is the woman?

FATHER: To those who are spiritually naive at this late date, the woman is Eve. To those who accept the teaching of the Popes, the woman is Mary, the Mother of the promised Redeemer. Might I say that text is what is known as a major prophecy.

A major prophecy is one containing words about a future event that are so clothed in obscurity that everyone who reads or hears them at the time proposed thinks they apply to someone or something of the time when they were uttered or written. In this case these words, think those, apply to Eve.

However, after such a prophecy is fulfilled, in looking

backward one is better able to understand them. Pope Pius IX said the "woman" is Mary. Her "seed" is the Redeemer, Jesus, and His followers.

BRIGHT: What does Mary have to do with it?

FATHER: The Book of Wisdom, one of twelve books the Protestant family rejected, but today put in the back of O.T. Scripture as Apocrypha, has this disarming text:

"And they knew not the secrets of God nor hoped for the wages of justice, nor esteemed the honor of holy souls. For God created man incorruptible and to the image of his own likeness he made him. But by *envy* of the devil, death [mortal sin] came into the world; and they follow him that are of his side" (Wisd. 2:22).

Mr. Bright, you asked what Mary had to do with it. The answer is, everything.

According to God's original plan, the Son of God made man was due to come into the world born of His virgin Mother Mary.

As we have already seen from St. Paul to the Hebrews, the Son of God in so planning to come to earth passes up the spirit world in order to be born of a woman.

This so irritated Lucifer and his buddies, according to Revelation 12:1 ff., that in their envy they blew a fuse.

It was this same envy that Satan (meaning false accuser at a trial) sneaked under Eve's skin, and Eve in turn got Parent to buy or "to eat" as it reads.

As a result of these goings on, God decided not to change His plans for coming into the world but was forced to change the mode of His coming, "found like man in all things save sin."

The word *sin* here refers to original sin and the urges to sin that come with man's nature at the time of his birth (fomes peccati).

BRIGHT: The Book of Wisdom says "because by *envy* of the

devil, death came into the world." I suppose the devil had little trouble in inciting envy on the part of Eve.

FATHER: You know your women, don't you? But let us remember Parent was equally as bad, if not worse. If you stop to consider you will quickly conclude that all the sins committed are in some way due to *envy*.

BRIGHT: Is this the reason Catholics put Mary on such a high pedestal?

FATHER: You've got something there. She is a pretty big part of the picture. Really, you know, with this amount of information, if one goes back and reads chapter 3 of Genesis it almost reads as if God were standing by waiting an opportunity to announce the coming of His Son through His Mother!

BRIGHT: Am I right in concluding that had there been no original sin, Jesus could not have come into the world?

FATHER: Here I must level with you. No Pope up to date has so declared. The smart boys (Fathers of the Church, theologians and many saints) are divided pro and con.

I happen to be on the side of those who claim Jesus would have come anyway, had there been no sin. It was this coming as man that made Satan envious. This coming would have been not as Redeemer but as Saviour.

BRIGHT: Why as Saviour if there had been no sin?

FATHER: You want to know something? No one today ever mentions this, but the spirits (angels) that never rebelled required salvation although they did not require redemption.

BRIGHT: Why so?

FATHER: Someone had to pay for the gift of their creation and sanctification. It was God who thought it up from all eternity about the creation. Logically He should have been the only one free to pay for salvation.

BRIGHT: God being God, if I understand this picture at

all, His coming into the world by way of birth from a woman must have rated Her rather high.

FATHER: Thank you for your splendid thinking.

BRIGHT: What purpose, then, creation in the first place! Would it be assuming too much to conclude that the entire purpose was primarily on account of Jesus and Mary?

FATHER: I'll buy that, and after that His love for the rest of us who are meant by God to become His and Her adopted children.

One must keep in mind that creation alone could not put one in heaven. Even God could not do that. God can't create God whence comes His likeness.

What God must do is to create a person, then move into that person to become one's abiding guest in order to create the presence of His likeness and divinity.

Such he did for the spirits and after them to Parent and his wife. God instructed them all and told them what the deal was all about. He also reminded them that they were free or had the liberty to retain God as their guest or to forget about Him.

In fact, Moses uses these very words: "retain" and "guard" (Gen. 2:15) the garden.

This was his chance. The spirits had their chance also, but Parent flunked out, as we know. He abused or misused his freedom, so God with His likeness vanished. All were sorrowful too late.

BRIGHT: Why does creation without sin require salvation?

FATHER: Creation put man (Adam and Eve) in existence on the created or natural level. God is on the level of the uncreated or the supernatural. For man to reach the supernatural level which is God, man needs God's condescending presence, which begets sanctifying grace.

Hence God has to take those He creates (angel or man) and make them over into His own likeness with His abiding presence. Or, as St. Paul puts it in several places, He created us to be His house, His home, His temple (I Cor. 3:16-17; 6:19).

"Christ in his own house which house are we" (Heb. 3:6). This is the heart to the entire game of life, the very purpose of our existence. What greater love! What can be more touching than for us in our body and soul united to be His "house!"

BRIGHT: It's too bad it is not presented that way more often. Am I to understand that the garden of paradise mentioned in Genesis 1, 2, and 3 is the "house" of their own souls?

FATHER: It sounds that way to me.

BRIGHT: Has the Church ever pronounced on the subject?

FATHER: Not to my knowledge.

BRIGHT: Why not?

FATHER: The Church (Pope) permits the people to have more liberty that way. It keeps them studying, learning more and more. In fact, when Jesus said to the good thief, "This day you shall be with me in paradise," was Jesus speaking of the paradise of his house or soul for which purpose were all men created?

The Church has never told us what the original sin was, except to say it was an act of "disobedience" brought on by the "prevarication" of Serpent.

Prevarication, to save you from asking, is a shuffling of the meaning put to words—something like double talk.

BRIGHT: Most people think the forbidden fruit was sex.

FATHER: We quoted Wisdom to show it was not sex but *envy*. Really, it matters not. We believe in original sin. What the sin was, we do not know for sure. But we do know that we are paying the price for it. Mystery? Everything is a mystery.

BRIGHT: I hear it said that when the Catholic Church gets

stumped on some point of religion, the first thing they cry is mystery.

FATHER: Instead of Mr. E., would it sound better to say Mrs. E.?

BRIGHT: A moment ago you stated it is your studied opinion that had there been no original sin, Christ would have come into the world anyway. On what do you base your studied opinion?

FATHER: The fact of His coming with Mary His Queen Mother even before Lucifer's fall was made known to the spirit world. If He wasn't going to come, why should His coming have been revealed to the spirit world in advance of their Fall? Read the letter to the Hebrews several times carefully and see what you come up with.

Those who hold the opposite view support their claim more or less from St. Augustine's famous dictum *"O felix culpa* [O happy fault] which brought Jesus and Mary into the world!"

To me those words do not show that it was because of original sin that He came. Rather they proclaim that because He did come the way He did after original sin, He came in fuller measure. Again I say read Hebrews in this light. After original sin Christ is our head. Before, Parent was. Is this why Augustine cried, *"O felix culpa?"*

BRIGHT: From all of this I gather that Mary cannot be put on too high a pedestal, since She is the Mother of the Creator and our Redemer and our Saviour and the occasion for creation as well as sanctification.

FATHER: Well said. Listen to a lecture on the heavenly galaxies and their astronomical numbers and proportions. If we stand in awe before the astronauts who reached the moon, which is only peanuts compared to the sun and Mars, etc., etc., what must be the immensity of God! What must be the stature of the one He created and sanctified to be His Mother!

BRIGHT: Am I to understand that this and more is what religion consists of?

FATHER: You better believe it.

BRIGHT: Well, then, if the Pope is not infallible we would be wasting our time. One can't afford to go through life wondering which direction to take, or living with a doubtful conscience.

Columbus stumbled upon the New World in his discovery of America, but even that was with the help of the rosary, so we are told, and one of the ships, the *Santa Maria*.

FATHER: So true. A true conscience is a dictator and we must follow it. A doubtful conscience is a nightmare, and who can follow it!

BRIGHT: So far, so good. Let me see if I have this thing straight.

We first use the Bible as a reliable work of history. By that reliable history we discover that God the Son, or the Son of God, became man. He was called Jesus because He who is, is to save mankind from its sins. We discovered from this history that He established His kingdom called the Church, whose charter members were the disciples. Of these learners He selected twelve to be *sent* officially to teach mankind or to bear witness to His revelations under the title of Apostles.*

As the Twelve preached the Word, God promised to fertilize it with His grace so that it might take root in the hearts of man. He so established His Church so that it had a president appointed by Him as the *Pope*, or *pappa*, meaning "head."

---

*The word *apostle* means "one sent."

Upon this head He conferred the office of infallibility as a court of first and last resort, as the case may be, so the people, both sheep and lambs, would know what to believe and to do, to follow the rules for the game of life, which is intended to be the taking-off field for heaven.

FATHER: Couldn't be said better. Thank you. But we can add on to that or should, in order to know everything.

BRIGHT: Where did the word *Catholic* come from? You know that's a dirty word to most people I run into.

FATHER: It is a biblical word. Watch this text. "*All* power in heaven and on earth [*all* over the place] is given to me. Go, therefore, *all* of you and make disciples of *all* nations, baptizing them in the name of the Father, and of the Son and of the Holy Spirit [*all* three Persons] teaching them to observe *all* that I have commanded you; and behold I am with you *all* days, even to the consummation of the world," for *all* time. The word *all* is used eight times. It is a Greek word meaning, in English, Catholic.

BRIGHT: You quoted Scripture to show that it was because of envy that death came into the world. Could this same envy still be in operation today?

FATHER: I heard a nice, clean, good Protestant Christian woman say that for the first time years ago. If you stop to think, the Church has been on the job for almost two thousand years. She must have enemies piled up pretty high by this time!

BRIGHT: I was thinking the other day about Vatican II and Pope Peter at Jerusalem settling Paul's difficulty. Do you suppose that must have been an ecumenical council in the Church?

FATHER: You guessed it. The Council of Jerusalem, it is called. And as long as we are now guessing, I like to guess that's where and when the Apostles' Creed came from. Of course, no one knows. As long as the truth is not out, one can guess or opine. But after the truth is out, then one must surrender all opinions. Have you given up some opinions?

BRIGHT: With the greatest of ease, now that I know that Jesus is really and truly God and that His Church is infallible in teaching the rules for the game of life and how to get to heaven.

It now appears to me that if I can believe some one thing that Jesus revealed, then I should be able to believe everything He said, provided the infallible Church so believes and teaches. This for the simple reason that everything or anything we know for certain, the Catholic Church has taught.

FATHER: You are so right. The Church was present from the very beginning. She ought to know. She has been alive from then, on down the years to the present time.

Protestantism at best came sixteen centuries later. How could they know? If I can believe some one thing on the authority of Christ revealing and the Church teaching, then why not believe everything (all) of the Catholic teaching on the authority of Christ revealing and the Church teaching!

In the last analysis any one thing that anyone believes must derive from the Church because She has preserved the Bible and produced what we call tradition (Luke 1:1 ff.; Acts 1:1 ff.).

BRIGHT: No matter what Christ would say, I'd believe it regardless of any previous notions, knowing that He is God. By the way, where does that word *Christ* come from?

FATHER: You know what the word *anoint* means, I'm sure. What is the essential thing about anointing or an unction?

BRIGHT: The ointment soaks in, but good.

FATHER: Well, when the divine nature soaked in, but good, into the human nature borrowed from His mother, the Bible refers to it as being "anointed with the oil of gladness" (Heb. 1:9); two natures united inseparably in the one Person of the Word. Such is the meaning of the word Christ. You know what? That union of the two natures was so close that when Jesus died on the Cross, God remained with the dead body on the Cross; and God remained with the human created soul when it went to Limbo. Isn't that something to behold!

BRIGHT: Then it would appear that the death of Jesus was as much of a miracle as was His Resurrection.

FATHER: In one sense that would appear to be sound thinking. That is the reason it is never said they *killed* Him, even by those who consider Him a human person.

He died sooner than expected because He worked the miracle of so separating the divine and the human natures that He, God, remained with His dead body on the Cross while he remained with His living soul when He descended into Limbo, or prison as Peter puts it (I Pet. 3:19).

BRIGHT: What does the word *Limbo* mean?

FATHER: It is a Latin word meaning "border line." In Hebrew it would mean hell. Peter clarified it by using the word *prison* so as not to think it was the hell of the damned.

BRIGHT: How come so many persons reject Mary? She was the first present when the Son of God was conceived. She was the last to be with Him at the Cross.

FATHER: A powerful question calls for a powerful answer. This goes to show the power of false propaganda, especially when taken with one's own mother's milk.

CHAPTER 5

Baptism—The First Sacrament

FATHER: If you recall, you answered negatively when I asked you if Jesus Christ had any existence previous to His becoming man in Mary's womb.

That answer spelled the doom of our Blessed Mother, were it true. It left Her to be an ordinary woman or person.

Little wonder that people list Jesus among human persons like the pagans Alexander the Great, Plato, and Aristotle, and Luther, etc.

This meant that Her Son was only a human person, and not divine.

BRIGHT: I'm beginning to see more and more why the Pope (Church) must be infallible in order to avoid a credibility gap in matters pertaining to His revealed truths.

FATHER: Quite so. Otherwise the old proverb would apply: *"Tot sententia quot sunt capita"*—"There are as many opinions as there are heads."

Do you realize there are over a thousand different kinds of religions in the world? That is not the whole story. You can speak to the different members of each religion and you'll likely get a different answer to the same rule. People simply believe what they opine or guess. That is not religion. That is not God's way. They had the same difficulty in Pope Peter's time. Read his I Peter 2:11-19. Who wants to go through life living in the darkness, as Jesus used the word *darkness* so often? He said such do not come to the light for fear they will learn the truth.

BRIGHT: How did Pius IX discover after nineteen centuries

that Mary was conceived in His Mother's womb without stain of sin?

FATHER: That was easy. The Church and all the people (Catholic) always so believed. It was in the Deposit of Faith.

BRIGHT: But Paul says to the Romans "as through one man sin entered into the world, and through sin death, and thus death has passed unto all men because all have sinned" (Rom. 5:12). Isn't Mary to be numbered among all men? And if so, didn't She therefore also sin, as St. Paul puts it, in Parent?

FATHER: Sounds tough, but really it isn't. True, all human men, including Mary, sinned in Adam as head of the human race, of which Mary is a member. However, it is the part of wisdom to distinguish; as Plato said, *"sapere est distinguere."*

Theoretically, or causatively, sin entered into the world, and thus death has passed unto all men because all have sinned, including Mary. However, effectively, or practically, sin (death) did not pass on to Mary, because God made an exception in Her case so She could conceive Her Son without stain of sin; so that the hereditary law of passing along said sin by generation to Him would in His case not be effective. Jesus thereby was exempted from that law.

Jesus is the divine Son, who ranks from all eternity. Even as man He is not subject to the hereditary law of original sin. He always referred to Himself as "the Son of *the* Man." No English text captures this nuance. But the Greek does. Of course, the Latin can't, because the Latin language has no definite article, as do both the Hebrew and the Greek.

When Jesus calls Himself the Son of the Man, He is referring to Himself as the Son of Parent *prior* to Adam's Fall, but not *after* it, as the rest of us are.

BRIGHT: That's terrific! Thank you so much. But how can

the Church say, as you do, that Mary committed no personal sins?

FATHER: Vatican II informs us that Mary's body was "formed of a special substance." She was exempt from the urges of the lower nature that prompted St. James to write, "Even the just man falls seven times a day."

At the same time She had a free will in order that She might play the game of life and thereby merit heaven. Perhaps these words from Revelation will add comfort to your mind: "And there were given to the woman [Mary] the two wings of the great eagle, that she might fly into the wilderness [solitude; in a class by herself] unto her place, where she is nourished for a time and times and a half time, away from the serpent" (Rev. 12:14).

The wings of the eagle are Faith and Humility. The time and times and a half time are the three and a half years of Her public trials:

She was the Mother of Sorrows when Simon's prophetic sword pierced Her soul.

BRIGHT: How does the Church know that Mary was ever a virgin?

FATHER: It belongs to the Deposit of Faith as a divine revelation. Ezechiel, 44:2, way back in his day so prophesied. So also did Isaias, 7:14, as did Luke, 1:27, etc., etc.

Catholic Christians always believed and still do, without a doubt, I hope.

BRIGHT: How about those who insist She and Joseph had other boys and girls later on?

FATHER: I can't be held accountable for anyone else's ignorant opinions. Again you can see our safety in the infallibility of the Church when it comes to what we must believe or not believe.

Always remember that faith, in order to be rewarding, never says, "How?" to God.

St. Jerome informed us that the brothers and sisters of Jesus were his cousins, the children of Uncle Cleophas, who was a blood brother to St. Joseph. It matters not to me who they were. The church says Mary was a virgin *before* the birth, *during* the birth, and *after* the birth.

I'm deeply conscious of the fact that God does reward me greatly for believing. That's the greatest private honor one can bestow on Him. What greater honor than to believe that I am my mother's son! Not even my father knows that for sure.

BRIGHT: But how could Mary remain a virgin while giving birth to a bouncing baby as Jesus must have been?

FATHER: (1) We never say, "How?" to God's doings. (2) Luke makes it clear that Mary did not agree to be His mother until She forced an explanation from Gabriel showing that Her promised virginity would not be impaired. (3) If the death of Jesus was as much or more of a miracle than His Resurrection through the stone tomb because of the divine nature which "melted" the human nature so as to give it new penetrating properties, why not see the same miracle in Her virgin birth, O ye of little faith! (4) Moses said in Genesis 3:15 that Serpent would be trampled on by Her. Is that not enough! (5) John says concerning His birth, we saw His glory—glory as of the only begotten of the Father—full of grace and truth (John 1:14) as he announces the Virgin Birth. (6) Luke states the "glory of God shone round," etc. (2:9). Are we to understand by Luke 2:13, 14-15 that angels were the midwives at the Virgin Birth!

BRIGHT: Since Mary was not tainted by original sin nor even by personal sin, did She require Baptism?

FATHER: Since Jesus, Her Son, is head of the Church as well as its king, did He require Baptism?

BRIGHT: I would think not.

FATHER: Would His Mother, His Queen, be the same? Actually the Church has never spoken on that question. Besides, it has no value for the rules for the game of life nor for us to get to heaven.

BRIGHT: Baptism, the first and most necessary sacrament, many claim to be a bit, or more than a bit, of superstition. How can a dab of water and words put God in the soul?

FATHER: Water always was, and still is, a scarcity in those parts of the world. People just don't live where there is no water. So Jesus, in setting up His seven sacraments for the seven main phases of a person's life in order to convey His graces to their souls, hit upon the easy idea of using material signs and words which He would recognize as well as acknowledge. These signs would tell the people what God is to work through this sacrament. Place the sign of water as applied to the person in any way and at the same time use the words which He commanded. God would see this as well as the intentions of those involved and God would come with His abiding grace to perform what was intended or asked for by said sign as He instituted it.

BRIGHT: Which are the effects of Baptism?

FATHER: First of all you must be informed that Baptism washes away original sin and all sins (personal) and all punishment due to sin. (2) You must be told that after that cleansing God comes and resides in that soul. This makes one a child of God, which one was not at birth. (3) You must remember it makes one a member of the Church. (4) As a member of the Church, only then is said person eligible to receive any of the remaining six sacraments.

CHAPTER 6

Confirmation

Confirmation is the next sacrament. It is administered by the imposition of the Bishop's hands and the anointing of the forehead with the oil of chrism—olive oil and sweet-smelling balsam—all of which is to remind the individual that his life is to be one of flexibility—athletic-like in a spiritual sense—and without stench but rather a life with the biblical odor of sanctity.

BRIGHT: May I ask what is meant when it is stated a sacrament is a sign that effects that which it signifies and signifies what it effects?

FATHER: If a little boy shakes his fist at someone, he's asking for it. However, shaking his fist may or may not start a fight. It does not necessarily start a fight. But if you pour (or immerse) water or apply water to some person's head with the words "I baptize you in the name of the Father and of the Son and of the Holy Spirit" with the proper intention on the part of the minister and that of the recipient, the sign effects what it signifies absolutely. The Trinity comes and abides in said person. He becomes a Catholic Christian.

It was stated that no matter who applies the water, the one on whom it is applied becomes a Catholic Christian and a member of the true Church, if done properly.

BRIGHT: Even if one does not so understand or believe it?

FATHER: Yes, indeed. Regardless of what youngsters believe concerning human generation, if they place the valid causes they will get the valid results The same for Baptism.

BRIGHT: How about those who use as the words "I baptize you in the name of the Lord Jesus" (Acts 2:38)?

FATHER: Not valid. Those are not the words Jesus said to use (Matt. 28:19), so says my infallible authority, the Church. What is referred to in Acts 2:38 is not how to baptize but rather the necessity of Baptism which, as stated several lessons ago, has the stamp of the Lord Jesus on it.

In the early centuries, even in the Acts, it is referred to often as the Sacrament of Faith; also as Baptism.

BRIGHT: Why?

FATHER: Because one must have the faith to know about and to receive Baptism and because it creates the eyes of faith in the person baptized, often called simply faith.

People who have never learned of the sacrament of visible Baptism might receive invisible Baptism, which is an act of love for God, as we saw above.

BRIGHT: I read some place, "without faith it is impossible to please God."

FATHER: You read that in Hebrews 11:6. Quite so. How could one ever come to learn the rules for the game of life if one did not believe them? By believing is the only way to come to know them. If a person is blind, he can't see where he is going.

Without faith one is blind. Unless one gets baptized, God will never come and dwell in his soul as his guest. God will never accept us as His lawfully adopted children—sons and daughters.

Jesus is the real, substantial Son of the Father because the substance of the Father is being communicated to His Son all the time. That kind of generation never started and it never stops. Such is the nature of God.

BRIGHT: Since Baptism creates the gift of faith within the person being baptized, how can he come to believe in Baptism if faith comes only at the time of Baptism?

FATHER: Excellent. You are thinking. The faith that comes with Baptism at the time of being baptized is called the habit of faith. This is called "habit," or a virtue, because it is permanently created at that time.

But the faith that one has which enables one to believe in Baptism, etc., is a passing thing. You read where God enlightens every man that comes into the world, and that those who received Him (Light) gave Him the power (willpower) to become the sons of God. May this example explain: If you went to a house after dark, how would you get through the dark house? You would first use a flash-light to find the switch. Then you would flip the switch. That would bring permanent light. Baptism is the switch that brings permanent light, Christ, God, our guest. May we keep him forever.

BRIGHT: If the Father has but one substantial Son, how can we become His children in Baptism?

FATHER: As St. Paul puts it, we become His children, adopted children, whereby we cry "Father" (Abba) and carry on communications with Him in our "own house." Thus was it He said to pray, "*Our* Father, etc."

BRIGHT: It just dawns on me now, the purpose you had in asking me the first day if we are God's children or sons when we are born into the world. I flunked that one too.

FATHER: You see; perhaps this is what threw you off. Maybe you had in mind we were God's creatures at birth. As such that would not entitle us to be or to be called his children.

In that widest of wide senses, cabbages and all the other creatures might be called his children.

BRIGHT: I don't suppose God gets any love out of cabbage heads.

FATHER: At least He does out of mine. But not much out of some of His people's. Anyone without God's abiding presence is not human.

BRIGHT: Is such a one inhuman?

FATHER: Yes, according to what Moses wrote in Genesis 5:1-2. It was not until after God had made Adam and Eve over to His likeness on the day of their creation that He called them "man." If it requires God's abiding presence to have His likeness and to be called "man," without his presence would not one be inhuman?

BRIGHT: Did it take all day for God to create and make man and the earth?

FATHER: The way the evolutionists hypothesize, it took Him a long, long time. He is still not through yet. The little Hebrew word *b'yom* can mean "day," "period of time," or "moment." The Church has never spoken on the subject. If you ask me as to mankind, I think God spoke and Parent immediately came into existence with God dwelling in Parent's temple. As to Eve, you know that story. And as for the animals, let the scientists have their day.

BRIGHT: That last statement sounded a little bit rough.

FATHER: It's about time someone got rough on that subject. Some teachers have been teaching strict evolution as a fact, since kingdom come. They do not tell their students it is only a theory.

BRIGHT: Does the Church teach any kind of evolution?

FATHER: Remember how you worded that sentence. No, the Church teaches religion, but not science. The Church states it is not against religion to hold mitigated evolution. This is the kind that believes in the existence of God, and that the soul cannot evolve even if the body does. After that the Church says go ahead and have your fun in dreaming about evolution. You will profit much if you read Ecclesiasticus 15:1 ff., 17:1 ff.

For a more adequate account of the sacrament of Confirmation, I suggest that you read Volume III of my book *God and Ourselves.**

---

*Published, in 3 vols., by Exposition Press.

CHAPTER 7

Holy Communion—The Sacraments

BRIGHT: It seems to me far more important to know with certainty where we are going and how to get there than to know where we came from and how long ago.

FATHER: Thank you for that statement; that is right up my alley. Or, What are the rules for the game of life and how to get to heaven with certainty?

BRIGHT: It appears we are arriving at such each day.

If God becomes our guest at Baptism, how do we preserve His presence?

FATHER: He left another sacrament for this very purpose. It is called Confirmation. You'll find it alluded to in II Cor. 1:22; Eph. 4:30; Acts 6:6; 19:1 ff.

Even if that were not so, we know for sure it is a sacrament because the Church declared it to be one of the seven sacraments mentioned in the Deposit of Faith. This Deposit of Faith is to be found in tradition.

BRIGHT: What is tradition? Is it the same as the tradition that tells us George Washington cut down a cherry tree?

FATHER: I'm afraid not. The tradition that tells us George Washington cut down a cherry tree is called a popular tradition—a story handed down by word of mouth. If he had cut down cherry trees by way of action from day to day and year to year, then you'd have a real live tradition.

Apply this now to Confirmation. Not only has the Church and all the people referred to Confirmation by word of mouth, since the beginning; what is more, the Church has been administering this sacrament since the beginning; as

Pope St. Clement said, "as has been handed down from the Apostles," and always so received.

BRIGHT: What purpose Confirmation?

FATHER: In Genesis 3:14-15 we read where the fight is on against the devil, who has sworn to become our house guest in preference to God. He won at the outset with Adam and Eve. So God, who took over the family of man later on, since their Fall, has left the seven sacraments in order to fortify man for that battle.

BRIGHT: If we need the seven sacraments now in order to get to heaven, what did Adam and Eve have?

FATHER: Genesis mentions one river dividing itself into four heads, or five rivers in all (Gen. 2:1).

I think the Church has never so spoken. That is a figurative way Moses had of informing us that a river of sanctifying grace divided itself into four heads or other rivers of grace.

BRIGHT: Yes, but there are only five, not seven.

FATHERS There was no need for seven at that time. They had no right to sin. Sin was never expected by God. So there was no need for the sacraments of reconciliation then as of now. Secondly, there was intended no sin or death to the body. In that case the Last Anointing would not have been needed. Sin and sickness are the results of original sin; therefore, Jesus, our Merciful Redeemer and Saviour, has blessed us with the other two sacraments to help man in order to get to heaven.

BRIGHT: I thought Adam and Eve were to get grace from the tree of life. What was it?

FATHER: God never said not to eat the tree, but "*of* the tree," which would mean the fruit of the tree, the same as we must eat the fruit of Her womb in Holy Communion. This must be the Spirit of Christ, which is the Holy Spirit, the furnisher of sanctifying grace.

BRIGHT: How would they partake of the tree of life?

FATHER: How do Christians and others today partake of
the Spirit of Christ since they don't have Communion?

BRIGHT: Then the tree of life is Mary.

FATHER: I have published a book that explains it, Mary,
Tree of Life and Our Hope.*

In the sacrament of Confirmation, God creates within
the soul of its recipient a certain equipment with which
to fight the spirit—the devil.

BRIGHT: You said God sent us to be His missionaries. Does
He have a sacrament for that purpose?

FATHER: You have hit the nail on the head. God expects
His missionaries to extend and to defend the faith by word
and example. This requires special equipment. Besides, as
we failed to mention when speaking of Baptism, he expects
us also to follow the rules for the game of life so as to get
to heaven.

In order to do this He infused into our minds and/or
our wills the gifts of faith with which to believe; the gift
of hope with which to persevere in looking forward to what
He promises, but which we cannot as yet see, for instance
heaven; the gift of love in our will whereby we can love
God above all things and our neighbor as ourselves. This
means to love all men regardless of who they are or what
they do to us, whether we like them or not, in order to
entertain our divine guest. We need that good will which
is lacking so much of the time. These three virtues are
called theological virtues because they afford the habit of
doing what is right by God (*theos*). The Bible says, "The
just man lives by faith." It also says, "Hope that is seen
is not hope." It also says, "Owe no man anything but to
love one another."

---

*Exposition Press.

Besides these theological virtues, God infuses with Baptism four moral virtues (*mores*: way of acting good):

1. Prudence, which is the sensible way to act.
2. Justice, which is the holy way to act.
3. Temperance, which hits the happy medium in all action and avoids extremes.
4. Fortitude, which is bravery, not to chicken out in the face of Satan's antics.

In order that the baptized person may perform well through any or all of the above-listed virtues, God at the time of Confirmation creates within the soul certain equipment of a spirit nature so that He, the guest, can constantly communicate His grace to these virtues. They are:

1. Wisdom: to do always what is in good taste.
2. Understanding: the light to see how to perform.
3. Counsel: the power to hear His voice.
4. Fortitude: His grace of encouragement not to be afraid—to be brave.
5. Knowledge: the grace of common sense.
6. Piety: His grace to urge us to be dutiful.
7. Fear of the Lord: so we serve to smell the dangers confronting us with Satan and his buddies, who are fallen spirits or his angels.

BRIGHT: That's a lot of equipment. It looks as if He has prepared us well for the battle of life.

FATHER: So He has. And for this reason did the cathecism used to read, "Confirmation makes us soldiers of Christ."

BRIGHT: Could that statement be misleading?

FATHER: Quite so. Since most persons, when they think, if they do, think with their imagination, at once they are apt to think of civil soldiers in uniform, ready for a war with killing.

BRIGHT: But it does not mean that, does it?

FATHER: No. It means to do battle in the uniform with the

equipment afforded us by Christ our captain through the sacrament. That is why Paul speaks of being "sealed" by the Holy Spirit. Also, that is why we need receive it but once. This is all spiritual and on the supernatural level. This sacrament should be received as soon as one has the use of reason, or sometimes before, because a child of God is held responsible for his actions as soon as he knows right from wrong. A seven-year-old is not immune from Satan's attacks.

BRIGHT: What is the point to that?

FATHER: It is the same as saying when one knows enough to push God out of His house so Satan could enter: love or sin—God or the devil.

BRIGHT: Is this to say or imply that when one drives God out of his soul by mortal sin, Satan enters immediately?

FATHER: Let the Scriptures answer your question: " 'But when the unclean spirit has gone out of a man, he roams through dry places in search of rest, and finds none. Then he says, "I will return to my house which I left"; and when he has come to it, he finds the place unoccupied [by a devil], swept and decorated. Then he goes and takes with him seven other spirits more evil than himself, and they enter in and dwell there; and the last state of that man becomes worse than the first. So shall it be with this evil generation.' " (Matt. 12:43-46.)

BRIGHT: You mentioned once that different chores are performed by God the Father, the Son, and the Holy Spirit. By any chance is this the reason the third Person is called Holy—because His chores are to make us holy with the presence of God within our "house"?

FATHER: You have said it. I lived a hundred years before I learned that from Pope Leo XIII's encyclical on the Holy Spirit. Sure, He is the forgotten Person of the Blessed Trinity. His chores are to operate the seven gifts of the

Holy Spirit through the seven infused virtues while building up within us the very formation or likeness of Christ if we but cooperate: God's own masterpiece of workmanship. (Gal. 3:27, 4:19; Eph. 2:10.)

"Come, Holy Spirit" should be in our thoughts as on our lips all the time. We are soldiers readied for battle with Satan to fight the game of life according to God's rules as we march our way to heaven.

Please, will you do something for our study for the next time: read John 6:1 ff, several times, then have some questions.

BRIGHT: I have always heard that an army marches on its stomach. After reading John, chapter 6, it sounds as if Jesus is preparing his listeners for the next sacrament, called today the Eucharist.

FATHER: Remarkable. It is also called Holy Communion. By it His lovers can communicate with Him who is love. You see, God the Son wrapped Himself originally in the flesh of man (the Incarnation) in order that He might appear among men and finally die in the flesh. Just before His death He wrapped His divinity plus His humanity in the veil of bread that His soldiers might eat him (love's union), and He still does through His priests.

BRIGHT: I read where many "walked no more with him" because they misunderstood the spiritual or supernatural nature of this eating. When they asked, *"How* can this man give us his flesh to eat?" it reminded me of Nicodemus, who said, *"How* can a man be born again when he is old." They lacked the faith, pure and simple. They were material-istic-minded.

FATHER: Of course. You also read where He said, " 'And they all shall be taught of God.' Everyone who has listened to the Father, and has learned, comes to me; not that any-one has seen the Father except him who is from God, he has seen the Father. Amen, amen, I say to you, he who believes in me has life everlasting." (John 6:45-47.)

Mr. B, you are being "taught of God" and you are catching on fast.

BRIGHT: I notice in that chapter that Jesus constantly uses the future tense, "the bread that I will give," etc. etc. When was the promise of the future fulfilled?

FATHER: You are certainly a close observer. Turn to Matthew 26:26 and read.

BRIGHT: "And while they were at supper, Jesus took bread, and blessed and broke, and gave it to his disciples, and said, 'Take and eat; this is my body.' And taking a cup, he gave thanks and gave it to them, saying, 'All of you drink of this; for this is my blood of the new covenant, which is being shed for many unto the forgiveness of sins.' "

FATHER: Do those words fulfill the future promise made in John 6?

BRIGHT: Nothing could be clearer. When He spoke of His "blood being shed for many," was this to signify, or to refer to, His sacrifice on the Cross?

FATHER: No one could say it better. Now turn to I Corinthians 11:23.

BRIGHT: "For I myself have received from the Lord (what I also delivered to you), that the Lord Jesus, on the night in which he was betrayed, took bread, and giving thanks broke, and said, 'This is my body which shall be given up for you; do this in remembrance of me.' In like manner also the cup, after he had supped, saying, 'This cup is the new covenant in my blood; do this as often as you drink it, in remembrance of me. For as often as you shall eat this bread and drink the cup, you proclaim the death of the Lord, until he comes.' Therefore whoever eats this bread *or* drinks the cup of the Lord unworthily, will be guilty of the body and the blood of the Lord. But let a man prove himself, and so let him eat of that bread and drink of the cup; for he who eats and drinks unworthily, without distinguishing the body, eats and drinks judgment to himself."

FATHER: Thank you. Any questions?

BRIGHT: Why does Jesus say, "Do this in remembrance of me"? Why didn't He say, "Do this in memory of my death"?

FATHER: Because He wished to be remembered by His life, death, Resurrection, and Ascension. He was born, lived, died, rose from the dead, ascended into heaven; he performed all of these feats for His soldiers—He the general, or our captain.

BRIGHT: How can some say He is not really present, since He said distinctly over the bread, "This is my body" and over the wine, "This is my blood," implying that the body and blood are both really present under the veil of wine!

FATHER: It's hard to say it, but when the dissidents after Luther lost the power of the priesthood, it was the next best thing they could say: "This reminds you of my body, etc." or, "This signifies my body, etc."

BRIGHT: Is this why some of your own theologians in Holland, I think it was, have been trying to do away with the age-old word (of Trent) *transubstantiation* and use in its place *transignification* since Vatican II?

FATHER: I'm afraid you've pinned them down.

BRIGHT: Is there any way they can be helped to save face in the ecumenical movement?

FATHER: The only way I can think of would be to say that before Jesus blessed the bread and the wine, these were a kind of memorial of Him and His last get-together with them. But not after the priest pronounces the words of Jesus, "This is my body—this is my blood," as Jesus' own representative. For Paul makes it pretty clear that if one partakes thereof unworthily, "he will be guilty of the body and the blood of the Lord" (I Cor. 11:27).

BRIGHT: You mentioned that the dissidents lost the priesthood. How was that?

FATHER: Well, when they denied the Real Presence, as I get it from history, the rite of ordination was changed to conform to that *memorial* idea thing. When they later on discovered their errors, many years later, they had no one left to pass on the real priesthood.

BRIGHT: To which error are you referring?

FATHER: The error that denied the Real Presence of Jesus under the veil of bread. The reformers used the words "This signifies my body, etc." They even so printed them in the Bible in place of the words "This is my body."

BRIGHT: Is there any Bible extant that contains such words?

FATHER: I'm told the library in Berlin has a copy.

BRIGHT: Those words are not found in any edition in recent years.

FATHER: That is right.

BRIGHT: When were they changed to conform?

FATHER: Many years later. When they discovered the error of their ways and rectified the reading in the Bible, they still preached their old formula, "This signifies my body," as many do still today.

BRIGHT: So the expression *transignification* appears to be a way of saving face and getting back in good form.

FATHER: Could be. Who knows what is in another's mind unless he expresses or explains it?

BRIGHT: I recall those words of Christ to Peter "The gates of hell shall not prevail." Indeed they gave it a good try (with the devil's help), but they failed. It will take a lot of humility (mental honesty) to set things straight again. Let's pray that they will come around. Maybe in another generation or two. They are on the way now.

FATHER: No one would ever guess it, but it is in the Deposit of Faith that all the words you read from Matthew and from I Corinthians is a performance or renewal of the sacrifice of the Cross together with the antecedent ceremony after the Last Supper. Today it is referred to as the Mass, or the Eucharistic sacrifice. Verse 11:26 proclaims this mighty revelation. So did the infallible church at the Council of Trent.

BRIGHT: Since Christ was or is God, what did He have to give thanks for?

FATHER: For His human nature. For His own Blessed Mother. For the grace He received from His Father to do, and to remain true to, the things He was sent to perform: live and die. People don't realize it, but Jesus required the grace of God for all of His human actions the same as we do, and He made use of those graces. He persevered to the end. The Book of Hebrews attests to this truth, but mightily (9:14).

BRIGHT: Is the sacrifice of the Mass the same as the sacrifice of the Cross?

FATHER: Trent says they are identical except for the manner of offering: the one bloody and the other unbloody.

BRIGHT: Why are there only ten words or commandments?

FATHER: If you read the Book of Exodus, you will discover there are many rules for the game of life. God has boiled them down into ten. These ten cover the main facets of life and those involved. The first three have to do with God directly. The last seven have to do with one's self and with one's neighbors in a direct way but with God indirectly.

The founding fathers captured the idea fairly well. When they wrote into the constitution the plank of separation of Church from state, they captured the meaning of our Lord's words: "Render to Caesar the things that are Caesar's and to God the things that are God's." Nonetheless, they did not separate religion from state. They wrote "man is endowed with certain inalienable rights: the right to life, liberty and the pursuit of happiness."

Here it is of historical importance, as well as of religious import, to know that the first draft contained the expression "pursuit of property" (wealth). Thomas Jefferson changed his first wording, which was irreligious, or if not that, at least amoral, to make it read as we still have it. The Holy Spirit must have been working on him. As we know so well, the possession of wealth may spell a certain amount of pleasure, but never happiness. Happiness too often eludes one. We never catch up with it fully until in heaven.

BRIGHT: What all is embraced in the pursuit of happiness?

FATHER: (1) To follow God's religion; (2) To serve our country; (3) To get married or (4) To become a priest or (5) To follow one's vocation, as well as some avocation, in life.

BRIGHT: Couldn't getting married come under the right to life?

FATHER: Do you think anyone would die if he failed to get married? In the pursuit of happiness marriage might fit well. For if one wants happiness even in marriage, one must work at (pursue) it.

Another reason for eliminating the phrase *pursuit of property*: this did away with the conflict with the Bible: "The desire of money is the root of all evil."

The bulk of the trouble in the U.S.A. today is the unjust pursuit of property.

BRIGHT: What about the U.S.A. being accused of imperialism?

FATHER: It sounds not so good, but when you realize who is saying it, it is not so bad.

BRIGHT: You refer to the Communists? How would you define them?

FATHER: A Communist is one who says, "What is yours is mine, and what is mine is my own."

We have many wrongs in our country due to private intrepretation and false liberty or a false idea of freedom.

Someday, either with prayer or with a catastrophe maybe, we will wake up and do penance as Our Lady requested at Fatima.

Was it Daniel at Nineve that preached and obtained penance and spared his city? Will we ever come to our knees in time to save the U.S.A.? O ye of little faith!

At this time I would like to ask you to obtain Pope John's encyclicals on *Mater et Magistra* and also Paul VI's letters; and you can obtain them from: Catholic Mind, 106 West 56 Street, New York, New York 10019.

CHAPTER 8

The Crucifixion—Redemption of Man

BRIGHT: To borrow your own words, if one had the eyes, or better, the ears of faith, one should see and hear Christ proclaiming the last seven words from the pulpit of the Cross.

FATHER: Couldn't be said better, unless you should add on that such might be construed as the liturgy of the word. Let us repeat them. This is not to settle definitely the sequence in which they were originally spoken.

BRIGHT: Do the authors disagree?

FATHER: They do. Offhand I would say not one of the Bible reporters even mentions all seven of the last words. Nor do they conform as to order. They select the words to suit their purpose in mind when writing the gospel that bears their name.

When hearing these words we recall that St. Paul informs us the first thing Christ did was to give thanks, from which word the original Greek for thanks derives untranslated, our very word *Eucharist*.

In periodic sequence during three hours, with ample time to meditate, came the following.

1. "Father, forgive them, for they know not what they do."

In this one sentence there reverberates the mercy and compassion of God. He informs us that anyone, everyone, always follows the mind under the guise of truth. One always alibis somehow to justify his actions. A poor excuse is better than none.

2. "Lord, remember me when you come into your king-

dom," spoke the "good thief" as he initiated the sacrament of confession at the Cross with true sorrow. Immediately Jesus gave the man absolution from all his sins. To show that the sacrament is effective Jesus answered, "This day you shall be with me in paradise."

Here we have a confirmation of what was stated at the outset of these pages, namely, that the purpose in the game of life is to keep God for our guest within our hearts during all our lifetime so that He may reward us with heaven. Earlier we referred to "house" in place of heart. Here He refers to paradise instead. Surely one's heart must be a paradise with the divine guest present and with the heart "furnished to every good work" by all the needed seven sacraments (II Tim 3:17).

Despite His sufferings, Jesus had time to leave an order with the promised woman of Genesis 3:15 to look after all His and Her promised children in these words:

3. "Woman, behold, your son," as well as to interpret what these words meant officially: "Son, behold, your mother." There stood the tree of life in person: She who furnished the Spirit of Christ. He was paying the price for sin by His Crucifixion, as revealed. He reminded all and sundry that hell should be the price and would be unless we repented and played the game of life according to the rules. To prevent our having to go there personally to pay the price, Jesus proclaimed for all to hear that He was suffering in our stead the pains of hell when He said:

4. "My God, my God, why have you forsaken me?" He was proclaiming what we are told by the Church, that there are two chief sufferings in hell: the pain of loss and the pain of sense. And what could be worse?

In this "last word" is announced the pain of loss, while in the next word to come He bespeaks the pain of sense or of thirst, each of which spells hell.

BRIGHT: Is this to say that Jesus, while hanging on the Cross, suffered the pains of hell?

FATHER: Nothing else but, as said above, He proclaimed the happenings in this His homily.

From Genesis to Paul and to John in the Apocalypse, the Scriptures equate hell with "death." Yahweh used that word with Parent when He gave sanction to His covenant with him, at the beginning of time (Gen. 2:17).

Paul used the word *death* several times to equate with hell: "He tasted death for all" (Heb. 2:9); "O death, thou are swallowed up in victory!" (I Cor. 15:55).

John, in Revelation, finally, after almost a century of confusion about the meaning of the word *death,* natural or supernatural, came forth with an improvement. He calls it the second death. (Apoc. 2:11; 20:6, 14; 21:8.)

When they informed Jesus that His friend Lazarus had *died* during His absence, He said, "He is not dead but sleepeth." Jesus on the Cross announces (Luke 11:11):

5. "I thirst." In order to inform all as He did above in (4) that He is tasting the thirst of Dives in hell, He uttered those words. Since He is God, in a moment of time He was able to satisfy for an eternity of time an infinitude of degree of suffering for all mankind.

BRIGHT: Am I to understand that Jesus went to hell for a moment of time in order that no one would have to go there in person forever if he played the game according to the rules of life?

FATHER: You could not be more right. Paul in Hebrews 2:9 states it graphically when he writes, "He tasted death for all."

BRIGHT: Right. A taste of anything is but a little bit. Jesus defined what He was tasting when on the Cross in the words of divine abandonment and thirst which He proclaimed.

FATHER: Remember this is the divine Person suffering through His human nature. This gives infinitude to all of His actions or sufferings.

BRIGHT: May I repeat how happy I am that you opened my eyes, at the start, to my ignorance about Jesus not being a human person.

FATHER: Thanks for your humility (mental honesty). This knowledge puts a whole new look on everything. It extends one's vision beyond words to tell.

Since Jesus from the Cross put all of us under the care of His Mother in those significant words, "Woman, behold, your son [children]," would you mind learning Her rosary and reciting it each day? That is to become your private line to your newly found Mother in heaven.

BRIGHT: I've been reading ahead somewhat, so as to be in better form as to what is to come. I note in the next word Jesus said with a loud voice,

6. "It is finished."

I recall you said each Person of the Trinity had certain chores to do. It appears the chores of redemption by Crucifixion are now finished as He yelled with a loud voice.

FATHER: Here may I point out an interesting fact? The words "loud voice" bear witness to the fact that He is a divine Person without saying a word. *Human* persons, after a little suffering, seem to lose their voice completely, or it is reduced to a whisper. Finally, with seeming great joy, Jesus shouts:

7. "Into your hands I commend my spirit."

BRIGHT: Does this mean to convey the revelation that the Holy Spirit from now on is to take over His own chores, those of salvation and sanctification?

FATHER: Precisely. His chores are the chores of santification attributed to the third Person according to the rules for the game of life, if one wishes to get to heaven. Paul put it this way: "By the grace of God I am what I am, and His grace has not been wasted."

BRIGHT: You agreed with my observation rather readily. Is there Scripture reference for saying the hands of the Father are the hands of the Holy Spirit?

FATHER: The Bible is full of them. In one place it describes a showdown between our Lord and His enemies. They accused Him of casting out devils by Beelzebub.

Jesus replied, as one gospel writer has it, "If I cast out devils by the *finger* [*hand*] *of God,* by whom do your children cast them out?" (Luke 11:20; 11:13).

Matthew refers to the same episode but uses an important change of words which should prove to you the point: "If I cast out devils *by the Spirit of God,* by whom do your children cast them out?" (Matt. 12:20).

BRIGHT: Then the finger (hand) of God and the Spirit of God mean the same thing.Thank you; you have proved my point. It's funny how often one can read the Scriptures and fail to pick up these points as he reads.

Pardon me. Did I interrupt your line of thought?

FATHER: Perhaps you slowed it down a little. I was going to mention that St. Irenaus, who was a disciple of Polycarp, who was a disciple of St. John the Apostle, who was a disciple of Jesus, said the hands of the Father are the second and third Persons of the Blessed Trinity, who operate in harmony.

BRIGHT: I remember you quoted Jesus as having said, "My doctrine is not mine but that of him who sent me," meaning the Father.

FATHER: Now you can add on to that a further text: "I came not to do my own will but the will of him who sent me."

Today we speak of a "hired hand" or a "hired girl."

The same difference so far as the word *hand* is used, meaning "servant." But Jesus did not like the word *slave* or *servant*. On occasion He said to His missionaries (Apostles), "I will not call you servants, but friends."

BRIGHT: In speaking of hands, hired hands, etc., how about the Blessed Mother and Her "Behold the *handmaid* of the Lord"?

FATHER: You are on the ball today. I was about to say that when Jesus said, "Father, into your hands I commend my spirit," that last word on the Cross opened up a whole new vista of thought. Mary was the Father's handmaid in person for the thirty years of Jesus' private life.

When She agreed to be the virgin Mother of God, She joined hands with the Holy Spirit forever. So when on the Cross Jesus said, "Father, into your hands I commend my spirit," Jesus was commending the salvation of mankind into the conjoined hands of the third Person and the Blessed Mother.

BRIGHT: Sounds right. He had just finished His work of redemption by paying the price with His life. He showed by turning His life off in death that He was not killed. He fulfilled His own words in John: "I have the power to lay down my life and the power to take it up again. No one takes it from me." (John 10:18.)

The fruition of that price, I now understand, is the work of salvation or sanctification.

FATHER: What is more, it makes Mary the mediatrix, or executrix, of all graces. Which of these words do you prefer?

BRIGHT: Since Protestants and non-Catholics raise such a fuss about calling Mary a mediator in opposition to St. Paul, who says, "One is our mediator between God and man," the tyranny of words might suggest *executrix* of His last will and testament, which is, "He wills the salvation of all men and that they come to a knowledge of *all* [Catholic] truth," or in another text, "He wills the sanctification of all men."

FATHER: Very good. But what would be wrong in seeing Mary as the mediator between man and Jesus, who is mediator between God and man? Besides, why would Jesus when dying on the Cross share His mother with us, to use His own words, "Woman, behold, your son; [Son] Behold, your mother"?

BRIGHT: It does not require much faith to discover that as our Mother she should distribute the cookies (grace) now and then. She gave a good demonstration at the wedding feast of Cana when she merely dropped a hint: "They have no wine."

FATHER: Yes; if you recall She said then the important thing is to follow His rules: "Whatsoever he shall say to you, do you."

BRIGHT: You have mentioned at different times that the Commandments, while mostly written in the negative, do have a positive aspect to them. Would that mean they encourage the practice of certain virtues?

FATHER: By all means. The first three look after the virtue of religion, which has to do with relating directly with God, as already stated. The fourth is solicitous for the virtue of piety, which involves all of our duties to our parents.

Inasmuch as parents or married people vote over (cede) certain of their rights to the government (or country), the virtue that makes one dutiful to his country is called patriotism. The Fifth Commandment, while proscribing murder and unjust anger, at the same time prescribes mercy, meekness, and clemency.

The Sixth Commandment forbids overindulgence in sex, such as adultery, fornication, all sorts of immodesty, impurity, unchastity, and incest or whatever involves a relative to the same degree as that which proscribes inter-marriage among them. Masturbation too is outlawed.

The virtues leading up to this control are called modesty, purity, chastity, virginity, and continency.

BRIGHT: Basically, might I ask, why is lust indulgence outside of lawful marriage forbidden?

FATHER: You'll find different explanations in various authors. Mostly, they suggest that if promiscuity abounded along these lines, responsibility would never or seldom rest where it belongs. However, it seems we can find a different approach.

BRIGHT: Is there a scriptural approach?

FATHER: St. Paul uses the words "their god is their belly." The belly is the torso. The torso houses the organs that are the seat of lust with their pleasure. To play a tune on any of the organs (erotic) for the sake of lustful pleasure is to invert the order established by the Creator for which purpose they were created. The lust attached thereto is to be a sort of guarantee or inducement to the performance of the ensemble required for the fulfillment of lawful marriage. St. Thomas with his philosophic mind would call it a deordination of reason. St. Paul with his mind attuned to the actions of the pagans referred to it as idolatry in his metaphorical statement already quoted.

BRIGHT: Could this not be said of the violation of any of the ten words of the last seven commands?

FATHER: Quite so. Lying, as most think, is not wrong because it deceives someone. It is wrong because it is a misuse of the gift of speech. So in the case of gluttony, do we eat to live or live to eat?

We may not invert the right order of any of the things that come from God.

BRIGHT: I've been thinking.

FATHER: I thought I felt something.

BRIGHT: What I want to know is this: It seems to me the
genitalia and all of the erotic centers form one vast complex in the human anatomy. This complex is a sort of built-
in equipment reserved by the Creator as the necessary
physical dowry to be exchanged at some future date—between an unmarried man and an unmarried woman as the
substance of their marriage contract should either ever so
desire in keeping with the will of the Creator.

FATHER: Well said, Dr. Bright. From this would follow the
Church's diriment impediment of impotency. This is to say
if either man or woman is found wanting in any of the
equipment needed or required for the purpose of marriage,
such a one would not be eligible for a valid marriage.

BRIGHT: Could there be included in this also that any intention or will to act on the part of either to prevent the
proper usage of this equipment, the marriage itself would
be considered invalid from the start?

FATHER: That is the reason why in the marriage interroga-
tion the following questions are asked: *(a)* Are you at-
taching any conditions, restrictions, or reservations of any
kind to your consent to this marriage? *(b)* Do you intend
to enter a permanent marriage that can be dissolved only
by death? *(c)* Do you intend to be faithful to your husband
(wife) always? *(d)* Do you understand one of the primary
purposes of marriage is the begetting of children, God willing? *(e)* Do you or your intended wife (groom) accept and
intend to fulfill this obligation? *(f)* Have you and your intended wife (groom) the intention of granting the other
the right to true marital intercourse? *(g)* Do you intend to
live according to the law of God which forbids sinful birth
control? *(h)* Are you aware of any physical defect that
would prevent you from performing the marriage act?

BRIGHT: It appears very clear that the list of questions,
eight of them, just mentioned, should indicate or prove

the point made, that the equipment is entirely out of the hands of each individual, so to speak; that no one has any right to use said equipment in any way other than God intended, namely, within the confines of a true and valid marriage.

FATHER: We are in agreement.

BRIGHT: Is there any other biblical text that would support such an unheard-of statement?

FATHER: May we fall back on St. Paul again for a rescuing act? He recited, "Do you not know that your members are the temple of the Holy Spirit, who is in you, whom you have from God, and that *you are not your own?*" (I Cor. 6:19.)

BRIGHT: What is the answer when "they" throw the old free-will act at you?

FATHER: Paul answers that too: "For a slave who has been called in the Lord, is a freedman of the Lord; just as a freeman who has been called is a slave of Christ. You have been bought with a price; do not become the slaves of men." (I Cor. 7:22-23.) This last text follows in the wake of Paul's pronouncement on matrimony and virginity.

BRIGHT: Does obedience to God's rules leave much chance to practice free will?

FATHER: Functional or physical free will? No. If you mean moral free will, then you have all the freedom in the world; the freedom to follow supreme truth, which alone makes not only us free but leaves God, who is Supreme Truth, to be free.

CHAPTER 9

Further Study of the Sacraments

FATHER: I think we already have cited this text from St. Peter, the first Pope, in his first encyclical. It won't hurt to quote it here in order to show that the devil acts on people in the case of either envy or free will.

"You must silence the ignorant talk of foolish men by your good behavior, but do not use your freedom as a cloak for vice. In a word, live as servants of God." (I Pet. 2:15-17.) According to Peter, we are truly free only when we are servants or slaves to the rules of life on how to get to heaven.

In speaking of Mary's power of intercession in one's behalf, what about the visitation with Elizabeth? Elizabeth informs us in these (paraphrased) words: "No sooner did you invoke the blessing of God upon me and my unborn child than your blessing did happen. My child leaped for joy, and I was filled with the Holy Spirit."

Indeed, She gave utterance to words that no man could have uttered. Imagine an old woman like Elizabeth sounding off in prophetic words that combined the major prophecy of Genesis 3:15 with the Crucifixion of Jesus some three years yet to come. How she picked up the refrain of Gabriel: "Blessed art thou among women" and repeated those same words (Luke 1:28, 42)!

Elizabeth was separated from the former (Gen. 3:15) by hundreds of years, and from the latter (Luke 1:42) by some one hundred miles. What greater proof do we need?

BRIGHT: The Eucharist and the Mass loom ever larger as we study them.

FATHER: Quite so. If you are much of a historian you will, upon reflection, discover that persecution of the Church has started with the martyrdom of the clergy, or their imprisonment. The Mass and the Eucharist are the heart of the Church. The devil knows this. Thus does he stir up the enemies of the Church, in order to do away with His priesthood, either by killing the clergy, as in China, or by striving to kill the Mass, as by the Volstead Act, which Satan engineered, perhaps unknown to others.

BRIGHT: Why does there need be a persecution of the Church?

FATHER: That's the name of the game of life. Jesus so foretold it. Satan in hell is envious of the sons and daughters of Jesus and Mary.

BRIGHT: Why, then, strive to have peace among nations if there "shall always be wars and rumors of war"?

FATHER: Pardon. Jesus said, "When you hear of wars and rumors of wars, do not be alarmed . . . the gospel must first be preached to all nations" (Mark 13:7-11).

BRIGHT: Mary, or the Blessed Mother as you call Her, begins to loom rather large from the Bible. I never realized it before.

FATHER: Do you see now why we are accused of Mariolatry, or worshipping Her instead of God?

BRIGHT: Is my face red?

FATHER: No. Why?

BRIGHT: Well, it ought to be for calling Jesus a human person. That's awful. No wonder people have forty fits about Catholics and their virgin Mother.

FATHER: Why?

BRIGHT: Well, if Jesus is only a human person like the rest of us, then His Mother shouldn't count for much. You don't see people making a fuss over anybody else's mother. Live and learn. I'm sorry for having been such a dunce.

FATHER: That was quite a confession. Without the eyes of
faith no one could see it, so thank God for the faith. As a
matter of fact, the next sacrament is that of Penance, or
confession. Since Vatican II it should be called the Sacrament of Reconciliation, which is clearly biblical from Paul
(II Cor. 5:18-19).

BRIGHT: Why do certain people poke fun at Catholics about
this sacrament?

FATHER: It seems to me Catholics do not bear sufficient witness to the beautiful things we have. We are rather poor
missionary soldiers. We do not brag enough about the mar-
velous things our commander in chief left us.

Just think, if a soldier goes AWOL or violates a commandment in a serious way, Jesus makes the first move to-
ward a reconciliation. Boy, you'll never guess until you
experience it what a wonderful experience it is, when one
has lost the Divine Guest to have Him return!

BRIGHT: How often can this go on in life?

FATHER: Jesus said until seventy times seven times. That
is a Hebraism or Aramaicism which would be in their language "as often as."

BRIGHT: Where does the Church get the idea that she can
forgive sins through the priest?

FATHER: It's all in the Deposit of Faith, so far as the essence of the sacrament goes. As to some details, that is left
to the Church to work out in keeping with the times. We
are experiencing just such an event during the present time.

BRIGHT: Is it biblical?

FATHER: (1) Yes. Does everything have to be biblical?
Which came first, the chicken or the egg? Which came
first, the book or its author? the Church or the Bible?
(2) Yes. St. Paul, II Corinthians 11:18-19, says, "He
has put in us the word of reconciliation." (3) The Church
informs us that Jesus requires the act of confession for

every serious sin—mortal sin, we call it, after the Bible—
as to number and species.

BRIGHT: What do you mean by *species?*

FATHER: Put it this way. Suppose someone confessed that
he was disobedient, etc. If that was to his boss or to his
parent, the species of obedience would change. Or suppose
you called someone a liar. The species of dishonor would
change with the dignity of the person dishonored.

BRIGHT: Oh, yes, I remember back in the days of Father
Coughlin. On the radio, before TV, he called Franklin
Delano Roosevelt a liar. His bishop made him get back
on the radio the next Sunday and apologize. He said, "You
can't call the President a liar even if he is one."

FATHER: Since you are digging up history, here is one. One
night I was lecturing the Klu Kluxers. This question was
found in the Question Box: "May a husband be present
when his wife goes to confession?"

I answered: "So far as I am concerned, her husband
and the whole relationship may be present. It matters not
to me. Now, Mr. Man—I take it that is a man who placed
this question—would you, Mr. Man, be willing to have your
wife present if you went to confession and confessed
honestly the things you've been doing? If you can answer
that question, then you can answer the one you asked me.
I imagine the question came from a man since the burden
was put on the woman."

BRIGHT: Why has there been so much "dirt" associated with
this sacrament?

FATHER: Satan got his oar in for propaganda purposes and
for prevarications.

For example, these dear souls heard some reference
made to the "secret" of the confession, as it has been called
for centuries. To Catholics the word meant secret of the
lips. To the enemy *secret* meant a secret place in the church

building where only certain women would go to be with the priest. Men, they said, never go to confession. Now you see the insidious idea that underlay that last question.

Was it not our Lord who said, "Evil to him who thinketh evil"?

BRIGHT: How often is one required to make a confession?

FATHER: As often as required to affect a reconciliation between man and God, so God will return to his "house" as guest.

If one understood the rules for the game of life, no one should be required to confess. Gladly should he look for the first chance after an act of contrition to get his guest to return.

BRIGHT: When did Jesus institute this sacrament?

FATHER: We do not know for certain, but we do know the Apostles received the power to forgive sins when they were ordained priests at the First Mass after the last Paschal Lamb supper. However, the jurisdiction to exercise that power was not given until after His Resurrection, when He breathed on them and said, "Whose sins you forgive, they are forgiven them and whose sins you retain, they are retained."

BRIGHT: What is jurisdiction?

FATHER: It is the conferred authority to exercise one's rights or powers. Let me illustrate. A lad graduates with a passing grade from law school. He has the intellectual and legal know-how to practice law. However, he does not have the jurisdiction in any state to practice law until said state grants him jurisdiction. Only after he passes the bar examination does he get the jurisdiction to practice law in any state of the Union or before the Supreme Court.

BRIGHT: I never knew that.

FATHER: It's worthwhile to discover that you are learning a little something in our classes.

BRIGHT: Did you say a little? I would say a lot. I never anticipated such a treat. Do you mind if I say there's a lot of false propaganda out about taking instructions from the priest?

FATHER: Sure. Our Lord anticipated as much when He was on earth. Read John 3:19-21: "Now this is the judgment: The light has come into the world, yet men have loved the darkness rather than the light, for their works were evil. For everyone who does evil hates the light, and does not come to the light, that his deeds may not be exposed. But he who does the truth comes to the light that his deeds may be made manifest, for they have been performed in God."

BRIGHT: What do the words "performed in God" mean?

FATHER: Recall, sometime ago we explained the operation of God's grace, which is playing the game of life according to God's rules. I think we mentioned at the time—if not, then let's say it now—a man must be motivated by the love of God in anything and everything he does (Col. 3:17).

Suppose you and I are marching down the street and some guy sees my collar. Of course, he'll make a beeline for me for a handout. So I flourish a dollar bill, then hand it to him with this intention: when Mr. Bright sees this he'll think, "Father is a good sport."

You know what? God never had a look-in on that deal. It was all self-love. No divine motivation. Nothing recorded in the book of life in my favor when I die.

BRIGHT: How about the next sacrament, the last Holy Anointing?

FATHER: When one is sick enough or old enough to die, he should receive this sacrament. If the priest does not volunteer to give it, when the time comes, then you demand it.

BRIGHT: Gee, but may one make such a demand?

FATHER: Of course. Since you have a right to it, demand

that right. If there is any doubt about it, ask the priest to give it conditionally. This is on condition you be sick enough or old enough. I'm glad Vatican II put emphasis on all of this.

BRIGHT: Is it biblical?

FATHER: Indeed, as is most every other matter that is bound up with the rules of the Christ for the game of life as preserved in the Deposit of Faith and taught by the Church. Please turn to James 5:14.

You know, people were about the same in the first days of the Church as they are today, meaning, "I'm from Missouri; you've got to show me."

The Bible does not contain everything Jesus said or did. According to John, "the world would not be able to contain all the books" (John 21:25).

What the Bible contains is mostly the things the people were hung up on. James' people were hung up on either this sacrament entirely or on one phase of the sacrament, namely, if one received the sacrament when unconscious which would take away his sins (granted there was present that abiding sorrow all should have always for sin), would the same person still have to make a confession if consciousness returned to him? James said in such a case yes, because we must confess all our mortal sins. Please read.

BRIGHT: "Is any one among you sick? Let him bring in the presbyters of the Church, and let them pray over him, anointing him with oil in the name of the Lord. And the prayer of faith will save the sick man, and the Lord will raise him up, and if he be in sin, they shall be forgiven him. Confess, therefore, your sins to one another, that you may be saved. For the unceasing prayer of a just man is of great avail." (James 5:14-16.)

How sick must one be?

FATHER: Sick enough you fear he may die, for example heart trouble, double pneumonia.

BRIGHT: What are presbyters?

FATHER: In the olden days the Bible translated the word by "elders" in the Protestant versions. The Catholics called them priests. Today both Catholic and Protestants use the word presbyters.

If you ask me, and you can take it for what it is worth, I think the word should translate "priests." I'll tell you why. In apostolic time life's expectancy was at the unbelievable low of twenty-three years. So whenever anyone was selected to be a priest, it must have been someone who was older and healthy. The Greek word *presbyter* means an elderly person, or simply an elder as he came to be called.

However, no matter what such a one is called, he still has to be an ordained priest.

BRIGHT: There's that idiom we saw before, "in the name of the Lord."

FATHER: It reads, "anointing him in the name of the Lord." Let me bring the point home to you in this way. Years ago in Fort Wayne an evangelist started his own religion in a tent. One day he stopped at a filling station to obtain some oil (crankcase). He told the attendant that he had read in James to anoint the sick with oil in the name of the Lord. He had a strong network on the radio, and was broadcasting that he would come and anoint the sick.

Well, maybe John D. Rockfeller's name was on that oil, but surely not the Lord's.

BRIGHT: Where do you get the oil that has the name of the Lord on it?

FATHER: From the Catholic Church, which He authorized to distribute such oil as is blessed by the Bishop on Maundy (the mandate to wash feet) Thursday, before Easter Sunday.

BRIGHT: "The prayer of faith will save the sick man." What's that mean?

FATHER: It means (1) the sick man accepts this simple

anointing with blessed oil (olive or vegetable) as a sacrament, (2) and "the Lord will raise him up": build him up. This explains number one above. The Lord will provide the grace in this sacrament to so allay all tortures of mind that the sick man will relax and go on and get well. This provided he gets this sacrament in time and provided a miracle will not be required as in the last stages of cancer, or with another proviso "that it is good for his soul right now," as some theologians say.

BRIGHT: "If he be in sins, they shall be forgiven him." I thought one had to go to the sacrament of confession for that.

FATHER: Right you are, but this is the case referred to above. In case one is unconscious, such a one can't go to confession. If he requires consciousness, what then? That was their problem. James said in such a case go to confession: "Confess your sins, therefore, one to another." The word *therefore* in that sentence seems to be the key word, while the whole sentence is a concluding answer to the question they were asking about without James' writing their question into the record.

BRIGHT: How about one to another?

FATHER: There would be no sense in confessing to any other than to a priest. This also includes the case where the sick person is a priest. Besides, it gives the lie to those who say, "I confess my sins directly to God." It really defines what confession is.

For example, I don't know how many times I've had people say, "I confess my sins to God," and not to some man. Always I ask them what God said in return to them. Invariably they would answer, "Nothing."

Take the word *correspondence*. One time a woman was bragging to me that she was carrying on a correspondence with Eleanor Roosevelt. I asked her what Eleanor said to her. She replied, "She never answers my letters." That is not a correspondence.

It takes two to have a correspondence. It requires two to have a conversation. And according to St, James, there must be two persons to have what is known as a confession: the sinner confessing his sin(s) and the priest, who alone is capable of forgiving the sin in God's stead.

James adds that the prayers of the (faithful) just man avoid much. It could be that the sick person is too sick at the time to pray. In that case those at the bedside might well fill in with their prayers.

BRIGHT: Over your fifty years in the priesthood, from which sacrament were you able to see the greatest visible results?

FATHER: If you mean visible to the human eye, I would say early first Holy Communion. It starts the child out on the love of God about the time (use of reason, 5 to 7) it has been weaned on the manifestation of affection by its parents. After that the Last Anointing has often been most pronounced. Of course, this sacrament is not comparable to Communion, because it is received less often.

However, one case comes to my mind. An old lady was yelling, moaning, night and day, day and night. No one could find out why. A Catholic woman stopped after Mass. "Father," she said, "you told us if we ever knew of any Protestant or Catholic that was dying, to let you know. Yesterday a neighbor woman was at my house. She told me of some other woman that lived still farther from her out in the country. Everyone was saying she was moaning because she was afraid to die. I figured, why not try the priest."

My guest told me the family had called every minister for miles around, but none could quiet her. I asked her name. I said, "I know that woman. She's a lapsed Catholic." I drove out at once to the home. The closer I got to the house, the louder her moaning sounded. It was horrifying. As I entered the house several married children by a first marriage (Protestant) were gathered around a rickety cot. I asked them to put her in a comfortable bed. I informed her I would be back the next day, Monday.

By that time the children from the first marriage had returned to their homes. It so happened that this dear woman, a Lutheran, had lost her husband by death many years before. She later on fell in love with a Catholic, an old bachelor. They were married out of the Church, for some reason or another, despite the fact she had been taken into the Church.

On that Monday morning I got her to stop moaning long enough to tell her I was bringing her Holy Communion. With that she said, "I'm a Lutheran."

Quickly I said, "Come, Holy Ghost, tell me what to do or to say." The answer came. I said, "Martin Luther was a priest same as I am. Could I start a church?" "No, you couldn't," she answered. "Then do you think Luther could?" She answered, "No." "If that's the case, then I'll take the sacraments from you." She confessed, received Holy Communion and was anointed. After that she relaxed and was at ease—no more moaning. I brought Communion several times after that. The first time I did, after that, blind as she was, she reached out to shake my hand, and she kissed the back of my hand. She called a grown daughter by the second marriage and introduced her and asked her to kneel down out of respect to the Blessed Sacrament. All was well after that. In a few days she died peacefully.

FATHER: We now come to the sacrament of Holy Orders.

BRIGHT: What does the word *Order* mean?

FATHER: The word *Order* means "rank" as among soldiers. If you recall, the sacrament of Confirmation elevates those baptized to become "soldiers of Christ" in order to extend and to defend His kingdom as missionaries.

This calls for the "battle of life" with Satan and his for everyone to fight to stay in the state of grace; to keep Jesus as one's eternal guest, and to bear witness or to give testimony to the truth of His revealed religion as explained, or as I have been doing with you and with others who have been deprived thereof in one way or another because of Satan's envy.

That being the case, there must be officers among the ranks of the soldiers. The first and important rank is that of deacon.

Deacon is a Greek word which means a missionary or *servant* who is a clergyman ranking below a priest. His duties are to preach, to baptize, to give Communion to the faithful, to witness officially a marriage as minister for both the state and the Church (in the U.S.A.) and to bury the dead.

The next in rank is the priest. He must have been a deacon elevated to the rank of priesthood with all the duties of the deacon, plus hearing confessions, offering the Mass and administering Confirmation in the absence of the presiding bishop, in the event of someone's sudden sickness.

Finally there ranks next the bishop. The word is biblical and means an "overseer" of a given territory or coterie of people. A bishop performs the same duties as a deacon and a priest and once held those two ranks, plus the ordination or the raising from the rank of deacon and priesthood to that of bishop. He rules a certain territory, or number of people who have no special territory, such as civil soldiers. His authority as ruler is restricted to whatever territory the Pope assigns to him.

BRIGHT: What is an archbishop?

FATHER: He is no more than an ordinary bishop, although he does have a little more authority than a bishop, as the *arch* signifies. He is ordered by the Pope to watch over the bishops of a given territory to see if each bishop is living up to his appointed standards. If a bishop should be sickly so as to be incapable, yet hopeful, of doing his work, the archbishop might recommend to the Pope that he be given an assistant called an auxiliary bishop.

BRIGHT: What does the word *archbishop* mean?

FATHER: *Arch* is from the Greek word *archos,* meaning ruler. Prefixed to the word bishop, it means a bishop who rules over the other bishops in a given territory assigned to him.

BRIGHT: Where does the cardinal come in?

FATHER: It is more an office of honor. The word itself comes from *cardo,* meaning a hinge. The cardinal, therefore, hinges, so to speak, upon the Pope's office and advises him, if need be, about the condition of religion and Church affairs in his own territory or country.

Sometimes this honor is given to the man, sometimes to the city whence he hails. The honor might be given, as has been done in the past, to a simple priest (because of his theological knowledge, etc.), or it might be given to a bishop. Today it is given mostly to bishops. History refers to cardinal priests and to cardinal bishops.

FATHER: The last sacrament is that of Matrimony. It is a union of a baptized man and baptized woman together with Christ. Its purpose is that of helping each other to get to heaven and also of begetting children and educating them for earth and also for heaven.

BRIGHT: You specified both parties to a marriage must be baptized if their marriage is to be considered a sacrament. Why?

FATHER: You should recall that Baptism is the first and most necessary sacrament. This means Baptism initiates one into the Church. One must be baptized before one is eligible to receive any of the other sacraments. In the event that one of the parties to the marriage is not baptized validly, their marriage is a valid marriage, all other things being equal, but not a sacramental marriage.

BRIGHT: Just what graces is this sacrament destined to give?

FATHER: I don't know if you are a married man or not. But we all know that marriage is not a lark. There are many, many problems too numerous to mention. For these purposes the sacrament furnishes grace.

What most people do not know and even those with a sacramental marriage do not realize fully, is the fact that the couple administer the sacrament to each other—over and over every time they make use of their marital rights.

BRIGHT: Why all this fuss about contraception?

FATHER: Let's put it this way. Do you like steak? OK. Then suppose you order a big steak. Along with the order you prescribe that the waiter cut the steak in small pieces large enough for one bite. To each bite you prescribe that a string be attached, while on the other end there be fastened a small tag numbered in sequence 1, 2, 3, 4, etc., or as many tags as there are pieces.

Then, when you come to eat the pieces you invert the numerical order to read 20, 19, 18 on down to the last piece, which would be number 1. Then, after you had swallowed all of them, you begin to extract the pieces starting with number 1. This would empty your tummy so you could have another steak.

BRIGHT: That would be gluttony if I ever heard of it. It is unbearable to think of.

FATHER: OK. Apply the same thing to contraception. It is too unbearable to think of. When a husband and wife become "one," they are inviting the Creator to perform His act of creation if the fertile time is right, yet at the same time you deny the Creator His right by an act of contraception. Is that praiseworthy?

BRIGHT: A good solution; I'm sold. Thank you. How many
of the sacraments can be received more than once?

FATHER: (1) Not Baptism. Once made a child of God, always a child of God, even if not in good standing. (2) The
same holds true for Confirmation. (3) Holy Orders falls in
the same class. It may not be repeated.

Let us put it this way. Each of the three aforesaid
sacraments so shrouds the soul with a certain irremovable
character that it always remains. If one should prove un-
true, then, as we learned already, such a one may be re-
stored to good standing by the sacrament of reconciliation
as often as necessary. Such is the mercy of God. However,
this is not to say that anyone may presume upon this mercy
of God. "Death comes as a thief in the night," so we had
better follow the rules for the game of life and live right.

As to Matrimony, you know it can be received but once
as long as one of the parties still lives. You want to know
something? OK. When people come to get married we hear
them say, "He [or she] is the only one for me." This is not
true. There are lots and lots of people who would do just
as well, because all men and women are created with the
same nature.

"He [or she] is the only one for me" should be said
after the marriage, and often. This would make them more
careful in their choice beforehand as well as in their mutual
behavior afterwards.

BRIGHT: I know the Catholic Church forbids divorce, with
remarriage. How do other Christians resolve their actions?

FATHER: They believe in private interpretation of the Scriptures. They misinterpret Matthew 19:1 ff. and kindred texts
to justify it.

I might say this: One time a Catholic boy and a Protestant girl came for marriage. I interviewed them and
sounded the girl out on her attitude about marriage lasting

"until death do us part." She said, "I believe in divorce and remarriage." I was shocked. Three times I interrogated her, in three different ways. Each time she came up with the same answer. Finally I had to say, "I'm sorry, but you are not after marriage as our Lord instituted it. Therefore I am not allowed to be a witness for Christ to the marriage. You don't want marriage as our Lord stated it. You want protection from or by the state."

They left. A week later they came back. She said she had consulted her minister in the meantime and that he told her, "In our church [of which she was a member], we believe divorce and remarriage is wrong but that would be the forgivable sin."

Our Congress has enacted laws sanctioning it. What can anyone else do! The same way are they sanctioning abortion today. Tomorrow it will be euthenasia or something else.

BRIGHT: What right has the state to pass laws about the rules for playing the game of life and for getting to heaven?

FATHER: It has no such right. It has usurped it. Such a right belongs only to the Church. Our false notion of freedom and liberty has given rise to many abuses.

BRIGHT: How does everyone get by?

FATHER: It is a case mentioned a long time ago about the use of physical or (functional) liberty in our country. We are only free to do the right thing. It takes a little thinking to swallow that thought.

If you listen to some of the popular orators on TV or radio, you will notice how they stay clear of such touchy subjects as the ones you ask me.

Pray the rosary so you won't be misled by Satan. It's the hot line to heaven.

CHAPTER 10

The Commandments—Rules of Life

BRIGHT: How are the rules for the game of life going to square with private interpretation?

FATHER: There is no true equation between them. About all we can do is to live with it and dislike it, while we follow the infallible Church. The payoff will come on Judgment Day for every single person.

BRIGHT: Is this why you put such great emphasis upon the divinity of Christ and the infallibility of the Pope as His mouthpiece?

FATHER: Exactly. This leaves one free of error if one follows their combined voices.

BRIGHT: What about population explosion and abortion as a remedy?

FATHER: Population explosion is a myth. I will tell you why. When God Almighty created the world with our first parents, He said, "Be fruitful and multiply; fill the earth and subdue it" (Gen. 1:28). That was a large order. That meant that God had implanted within the very bowels of the earth ample potential to care for mankind, as many as shall be multiplied, according to God's order. That is to say, there shall ever be ample potential to feed the so-called population explosion.

BRIGHT: It would appear that if little Japan can care amply for a population about one half that of the U.S.A., and on rather rocky terrain, then surely America can do likewise with all of its miles and miles of acres.

FATHER: I appreciate your observation. May we keep in mind that our faith in God and His providence, of which we are a part, need not violate any of the Commandments nor any of the rules for the game of life as we earn our salvation. God will never be found wanting. May it never be said of us that we are found wanting.

BRIGHT: It's been on my mind a long time: When God gave the Decalogue to Moses, is this to say that the Ten Commandments never existed prior to that event?

FATHER: It is to say they never existed on two tablets of stone prior to that time. However, the same as the existence of God, the Commandments were written in the "fleshy tablets" of men's hearts at the time of each one's birth (II Cor. 3:3).

Everyone knows that the Jewish people were the "chosen" people of God. Their sojourn for 430 years in Egypt with the pagans caused them to neglect and even to forget the Ten Commandments almost entirely.

The civilization of the Egyptians operated along the lines of private interpretation. Each village conceived and operated by its own rules. Hence were they called pagans. *Pagan* in Greek means a small village.

It was stated above that God's rules for the game of life were almost forgotten. To their credit be it said the Israelites did retain some semblance of an idea of the one true God, even though they did worship many false gods. Polytheism, it was called.

In the meantime the Commandments were effaced from most everyone's heart. In divine irony God wrote the Decalogue on two tablets of stone. Then God defied the Israelites to forget the rules for the game of life.

If my calculations are right, there were about seventy-two persons with Abraham and his children and their wives who entered Egypt during the great famine. These multiplied into almost two million by the time Moses and Aaron led them through the Red Sea district on to dry land.

BRIGHT: Some say that is a myth, that it was a strong wind that blew the sea back at the seashore permitting their passage.

FATHER: A strong wind cannot so divide the water that water served as a bannister on each side of the drive. I've heard that too. I recall some years ago the water at Lake Erie, next to Toledo, was blown eastward until the bottom showed. But this description is different, and it runs separately in the Psalms, Exodus, and elsewhere.

BRIGHT: The word *decalogue* is what?

FATHER: We started out with "the Word" (*Logos*). Here we are with it prefixed by the word for "ten." "The ten words"—meaning the Ten Commandments. One time Jesus said to Satan, "Not by bread alone does man live but every word that cometh out of the mouth of God" (Matt: 4:4).

Somewhere we read, "The word is like a two-edged sword" (Heb. 4:12; Eph. 6:17).

BRIGHT: At the outset we learned that the word is the spoken thought coming from the heart of the speaker. Does this apply here?

FATHER: Certainly. The Decalogue is the ten spoken words from the will of God meant to be the rules for the game of life on how to get to heaven. Jesus referred to them frequently. They still have binding force.

BRIGHT: It has occurred to me several times, and now I am reminded of it again: Jesus, in giving Simon Peter the keys to the kingdom of heaven—was that the authority to make laws having a binding force or sanction?

FATHER: Yes, and since He used the word *keys,* in the plural, He was referring to the other time this delegated power might be used, namely, in confession: "forgiving and retaining sins." I might add that whenever the Church makes a law, that law has as its foundation some doctrine or law growing out of the Ten Commandments.

Have you ever seen the picture of a Pope with two keys in his hand?

BRIGHT: Yes, I have. May I ask what *retain* means?

FATHER: First of all, the two keys are symbolical of this twofold authority in the Church to which we already referred: absolving from and making laws. To *retain* means more than the newest Protestant version has it. They use the word *unforgiven*. The new Catholic text has, "if you hold them bound they are held bound." "Retain" is a stronger expression than either of these two. Perhaps a slang word or the language of the street would say it better, as is so often the case.

If one confesses and refuses to promise to give up his attachment to some sin confessed, the priest in whom "Christ has entrusted the ministry [word] of reconciliation" (II Cor. 5:18) and through whom Christ (God) operates, rather than forgive that person his sin, will pronounce this judgment upon him: since you refuse to be reconciled to Christ, you are now "stuck with your sin."

BRIGHT: What about this late talk concerning the procedure way back when the Catholic Christians appeared in various forms, and weeping as they confessed their sins to the people upon entering the Church?

FATHER: That is reliable history. Some would like to introduce that into the present procedure.

BRIGHT: Why was it so done in the early days?

FATHER: Because when one sins, usually the sin, while always being an offense against God, is also a sin against one's fellow men, or the people of God. It was left for the people of God first to forgive the sinner and then for the priest to forgive him in God's stead.

BRIGHT: Why was it ever changed?

FATHER: Everything must change, and usually does, with the march of time.

BRIGHT: Who forgave the sins against the people of God
when that practice was discontinued?

FATHER: The priest did. He presided in the place of God
(Christ), as well as in the place of the people. You see,
religion is how to relate with God and with the people.
As we have been saying all along, everyone must play the
game of life according to the rules if he is to get to heaven.

The rules are the same for all. It is in the confessional
that these rules can best be expressed. At times one may
have an erroneous idea concerning some rule pro or con.
He needs to be set right. The priest will or should do just
that.

BRIGHT: Is this to say or imply that the priest is a sort of
lawyer?

FATHER: He is lawyer both for God and for the people of
God. For this was he prepared (taught) and sent. The es-
sentials of this sacrament have always been preserved. As
to the accidentals, they may change with the needs of the
times.

Some feel today there is such a need. I wouldn't know
because of the prejudice of people as I know people. Let
the Pope with his bishops decide with the help of the "experts," whoever they may be.

BRIGHT: What does it take to be an "expert"?

FATHER: I've often wondered. You tell me. Perhaps it is
one who knows not whereof he speaks, and neither does
anyone else.

BRIGHT: I have a pretty good notion about the Ten Commandments. Is there any point you would like to raise for
my benefit?

FATHER: Yes; the second one says not to take God's name
in vain.

Most people think that means primarily the misuse of

any of the names referring to God in their everyday conversation.

BRIGHT: What, then, is the extent of that law?

FATHER: It refers to anything Christ said which has His name upon it. We saw the expression several times, as used in the Bible, "in the name of the Lord." That is to say, sins against faith. Anything our Lord proposed for our belief has His name upon it. If you recall, we likened it to General Motors. This company stamps "G.M." on any and all of its products.

BRIGHT: That's one that is sobering. Any others?

FATHER: The wording "Honor your father and mother, etc."

The first meaning of the word *honor* is money, according to St. Jerome. How many people give money to their parents in time of need! Our civil government had to enact social security legislation because of a failure to obey this law.

BRIGHT: How about a text or two to substantiate your statements?

FATHER: St. Paul writes, "Honor widows who are *truly* widowed. But if a widow has children or grandchildren, let these first learn to *provide* for their own household and make some *return* to their parents, for this is pleasing to God" (I Tim. 5:3-4).

BRIGHT: That's pretty plain. St. Paul's text seems to outlaw divorces. Such are not truly widowed.

FATHER: Here it is not to be understood that every place in the Bible where the word *honor* is used it is to be equated with money. Sometimes it refers to honor in the sense of respect or glory.

There is a text that has to do with money to the Church: "He who does not honor the Son [in His Church] does not honor the Father" (John 5:23).

There is also a text that refers to the priest and his salary: "Let the presbyters who rule well be held worthy of double honor, especially those who labor in the word and in teaching. . . . The laborer is worthy of his wages (I Tim. 5:17-18)."

BRIGHT: What does double honor mean?

FATHER: Probably a living wage, but not double pay or time-and-a-half pay. Webster defines *honorarium* in about the same light.

BRIGHT: Very enlightening! Any more?

FATHER: Yes, "not to bear false witness." This means more than not to tell lies. It forbids speaking even the truth when damage might be done thereby, for example to speak the truth which could or would harm another in his business or reputation, etc. Recall how little is recorded in the Scriptures about the private life of the Holy Family, and how most every one bemoans the fact. They seem never to have heard about the virtue of *silence*. The Holy Family is our model in this too.

Example: I once heard a man complain, "I went to confession to Father So-and-So and he had the audacity to ask me if I was married." That stupid remark opened up to me what the nature of his sin may have been. For if one sins against chastity, he at the same time sins against his own spouse because his body after marriage belongs to his spouse. It belongs to his spouse because he exchanged his body for that of his spouse, which is the substance of the marriage contract. He had better keep quiet. In such a case there would have been a new species of sin. As a matter of fact, the genitalia and kindred erotic centers never did belong to the individual to possess as his own, but to be used in the process of exchange as already set forth previously, this exchange to be or to have been the substance of the marriage contract of which or to which

God Almighty is a most important partner. For a complete analysis of this point read my book *Mary, Tree of Life and Our Hope.*

The following two sections are for the reader's welfare.

These are the outstanding items of the rules for the game of life growing out of the Decalogue that most people fail to recognize.

BRIGHT: They certainly are. I don't think I ever heard of them before. How about the creed?

FATHER: If you take the Apostles' Creed, the creed drafted by the Council of Nice (4th century) and so named, plus that of St. Athanasius, called the Athanasian Creed, you'll get the bulk of the revealed truths that we must believe.

Paul VI in July, 1963, gave an up-to-date version or rendition of the creed in words that give the lie to any of the vaporings of present-day misguided people.

BRIGHT: How about holy water, etc., and some other practices in the Catholic Church?

FATHER: The Church is the spouse, or bride, of Christ, as we believe and know. What the Church prays for to God, her spouse, she obtains.

So when the Church prays through her priest, she prays that those who use this blessed water with faith in the prayers of the Church may be protected from the devil.

By the way, it was from a Protestant that I first heard the expression "I hate him like the devil hates holy water."

BRIGHT: I thought we were not allowed to hate our neighbor but to love everyone regardless?

FATHER: I did not mean the hatred of one's neighbors as expressed was OK but rather the hatred for holy water on the part of the devil.

People should have it in their homes. They should sprinkle it around the home and their offices too, if they have one.

BRIGHT: How about blessed palms on Palm Sunday?

FATHER: These things you bring up are called by the name
of sacramentals. Christ did not leave them for us, but the
Church, in imitation of Christ, and His sacraments, whose
bride she is, instituted them. If you wish to know their
value, then take the book the priest uses and read the words
of the prayer. This will inform you for what purpose they
are intended to be used by the people of God.

It should be added here that Palm Sunday is not only
the day on which palms are blessed. It is also the day that
commemorates Christ's triumphant entry into Jerusalem.
It was the Sunday before His Crucifixion. That day brings
back memories of His riding on the two donkeys (not at
the same time, however), the one old and the other her
foal.

This was a way of announcing that the Old Testament
gave way to the New—the old donkey in favor of the young
one, the way the New Testament came from the Old.

When Jesus died on the Cross, the veil of the Temple
in Jerusalem was torn from "top to bottom." This signified
that the Old Testament religion was unfrocked in favor of
the New Testament religion that began with the sacrifice
of the Mass, which was and still is the same as the sacrifice
of the Cross except as to the manner of offering: the one
bloody and the other unbloody.

Palms were blessed as a protection against storms and
cyclones, etc. You know what? Some years ago a cyclone
struck at my house, and every house in the neighborhood
was spared save one which was demolished. It was occupied
by a Catholic family who were careless Catholics and had
no blessed palm in it. A half dozen of the others were all
occupied by good Catholics. They were spared even though
surrounded by large fallen trees.

One time I read in the paper that the army worms were

on the march. They were so thick that as they crossed the highway it was dangerous to drive automobiles. Thus went the warning in the media.

I went out and blessed my people's farms. You know what? It stopped them. This is what shook me. The prayer read, "May they never return *until there is need for them again, etc.*" Then I sprinkled the fields with holy water.

BRIGHT: These prayers must depend largely on the faith of the priest and the people of God, according to what you say.

FATHER: That is quite correct. See what the people outside the Church are missing?

The sacraments *produce* God's grace, etc. The sacramentals (meaning: little sacraments) *procure* God's blessings.

BRIGHT: What, in your estimation, are the greatest things in the Catholic religion?

FATHER: It won't hurt to repeat the answer to this question.

No doubt the presence of our Lord in the Blessed Sacrament of the Mass and the altar come first. Then I would say daily devotion to the Blessed Mother in Her rosary. The two might be looked upon as *one* because it was when Jesus was on the Cross, right before He died, that He consigned His Blessed Mother to be our Mother, spiritual Mother, that is, and to distribute His blessings.

This, we learned, was when He said "Woman, behold, your son" and "[Son] Behold, your mother."

I notice that the latest Protestant text reads, "Mother, behold, your son." That is not a faithful translation from the Greek. It does, however, render the faithful meaning. Quite an admission for the Protestants to make, namely, that Mary is our Mother.

BRIGHT: Which would be next?

FATHER: You'll be surprised, perhaps, at this one. It's that of papal infallibility. For those outside the Church, each one is his own Pope. He may be right and he may be wrong in what he thinks or decides. As for the people of God, they can rest secure that they are always right in believing if the Church has given an answer.

BRIGHT: What if the Church has not given an official pronouncement?

FATHER: Then a Catholic is left free to follow his own thinking, but only in such a case, if and until a definition is given.

BRIGHT: How about how long a person remains in Purgatory?

FATHER: Such is not in the Deposit of Faith. So the Church can make no pronouncement on such a subject. The Church has no authority over the Church suffering. It is better to live by the rules that will take us to heaven and not to build up any false hopes.

Some Catholics are heard to say, "Just so I escape hell I won't mind going to Purgatory." They will change their minds if they ever go there.

BRIGHT: There is one more question I would like to ask. How about the sin that cannot be forgiven in this life nor in the life to come?

FATHER: Please turn to Matthew 12.31: "Every sin and blasphemy shall be forgiven to men; but the blasphemy against the [Holy] Spirit *will not* be forgiven." Note well, Matthew does not say said sin *cannot* be forgiven, but *will not* be forgiven.

If I translate my Greek text correctly, it reads, "Every sin of the spirit [devil] against the [Holy] Spirit *will not* be forgiven." This indicates the fight is still on.

BRIGHT: What might a sin of blasphemy be?

FATHER: Surely if one deliberately refuses to believe what God has revealed, that would be a blasphemy of the spirit against the Holy Spirit. It would be the same as to tell God He is a liar. Wouldn't you consider that a blasphemy of the spirit (devil) against the Holy Spirit, whose chores are to so inspire us to follow the rules for the game of life and how to get to heaven! If one blasphemes against the Holy Spirit, that person is attacking the very source of grace.

BRIGHT: What would you say is the greatest single factor missing in playing the game of life?

FATHER: The failure to accentuate love for God rather than drumming away at sin most of the time. His love must come from Him in a special way. It is divine love, not human love. It might be put in another way: too much love for the almighty dollar instead of love for Almighty God.

Stressing the positive is far more important than harping on the negative all the time, such as don't, don't, don't, though there are times when the *don't* should be stressed.

About the first thing our Lord did, as recorded in Matthew 4 ff., in His Sermon on the Mount was to give a new edition of the Decalogue under the title of the Eight Beatitudes. These are a positive rendering of the Decalogue.*

Later in Life He spoke the Decalogue to those to whom *don't* best applied.

BRIGHT: Why lay so much stress on His Mother, Mary?

FATHER: As said previously, the very magnitude of God removes Him an infinite distance from us.

The very abstract idea of God in His immensity baffles us because we are accustomed, day by day, to think in terms of pictures. Who can picture God?

He knew that, so He came in the form of man—very condescending—with His Mother announcing the key word when She said, "Behold the servant [handmaid] of the Lord."

---

*Consult my books, *God and Ourselves,* for a fuller explanation.

What else is this than to inform us that She is to be His servant and ours in His and our behalf?

In speaking of love, how often is it brought home to us that God created us for no other reason than that we be His own house for a love affair (tryst) with Him and Her here on earth and hereafter in heaven?

In answer to your final question Mr. Bright, I append the following sections. Consult *Mary, Tree of Life and Our Hope,* to which I have previously referred.

CHAPTER 11

Why We Pray to Mary

By this time the reader must be thoroughly saturated with the truth that Jesus is very, very human (but not inhuman), yet is not a human person (John 1:15; 31), but the divine Person of the Word.

In keeping with the fact that He and His mother are human, we come to understand Him, and Mary, so much better, because we too are human—or are we! He took the same nature we have but "without sin." Now, that deal He got from the serpent in the beginning? His being human, therefore, suggests one thing that we as human beings know. We have learned that in the association of ideas, memory is born. And if one has a mind to it, one can find very many places in the New Testament Scriptures, where our Lord is speaking, that He seems ever to have His memory alerted by the proceedings in the Garden of Eden.

Take, for instance, in the beginning of the drama with the "twelve." He spoke in deep tones by saying implicity that while Satan gained the victory over the kingdom of Parent through original sin, believe me, Serpent should never *"prevail"* against His kingdom.

Again, did He not say, "I come to save that which was lost"! And does He not refer to original sin (John 5:25) when speaking of passing "from death to life"?

Does He not confide, "The prince of this world [the devil] approaches. He has no *rights* over me" (John 14:31)? Is this not another way of saying that Jesus is the Son of the Man and not a son of Adam, the original sinner?

Association of ideas does bring back memories, and what memories! In John 15:1, Jesus says His Father is the "gardener" in this His new spiritual kingdom. In the old kingdom Parent was the gardener, only for a while, charged "to guard and to retain it" (Gen. 2:15). Parent flunked out. Jesus will stay loyal. So will His subjects (John 1.12). So did Mary; She proved that. What a Mother! "She stood 'neath the Cross."

That this is a spiritual garden and not a material garden, Jesus tells us when He says you must be reborn from above in order to enter it (John 3:3 ff.), and to owe our allegiance (John 1:13).

In Genesis the metaphor is on "sprouting trees," etc., while Jesus speaks of being the vine. He also alludes to trees (Matt. 13); Moses speaks of the [fruit of the] "tree of life." Jesus refers to the "fruit of the vine." Elizabeth says such "botanical" fruit out of metaphor is, literally, to use biological language, the fruit of Mary's womb.

In John 15:25 we read, "They hated me without reason." Behold, memories of Psalms 34:19; 68:5; Isaias 14:12 ff.; Genesis 3:15! So the same hatred arose because of Mary His Queen Mother!

In His closing prayer Jesus prayed, "For thou hast made him sovereign [commander in chief] over all mankind to give eternal life to all whom thou hast given him."

That is, Jesus, or Yahweh, in place of Parent, who failed, He the "seed of the woman" (Gen. 3:15).

Since He is the "fruit of Mary's womb," She is the Mother of the Redeemer and "Mother of all whom thou hast given me" (John 15:1; Gen. 3:15).

When Jesus on various occasions greeted His Apostles with the words "Peace be to you," was He not but speaking the words His Mother had taught Him throughout His whole life from infancy on (John 2:51-52)!

Jesus always used the same words as Mary did when greeting Elizabeth. It was from Her He learned them: "Peace be to you."

When Jesus in John 16:33 says, "I have conquered the world," is this not a fulfillment of Genesis 3:15, and Mary had Her share therein: He, Her "seed"! By "world," Jesus meant the world of Satan.

Jesus also said, "When the Advocate [lawyer] comes, he will tell only what he hears" (John 16:7; 13:23). We have already learned that Mary is joined, hand in hand, with Him. So we refer to Her also as our "Advocate." She who dubbed Herself His servant must be our willing servant too. Hence we go to Her with our prayers (Luke 1:38).

When St. John wrote that the "Word was made flesh" (John 1:14), he was but corroborating the words of Gabriel (Luke 1:31, 34, 35) and also the words of Elizabeth (Luke 1:43, 44), namely, that the divine Person of the Word took to Himself a human nature and was the "fruit of Mary's womb" (Luke 1:42).

When St. John wrote, ". . . and the Word dwelt among us and we saw his glory, such glory as befits the Father's only Son, full of grace and truth" (John 1:14), he was but declaring the Virgin Birth.

When John the Baptist cried aloud, "This is the man I meant when I said, 'He comes after me, but takes rank before me,' for before I was born, he already is" (John 1:15, 31), the Baptist was announcing that He is the divine Person of the Word existing from all eternity.

When Jesus said, "We worship what we know" (John 4:22-23) and "You Samaritans worship what you do not know," then went on to say God must be worshipped in spirit and truth, He was but adding on to the worship that must be paid to God the Father, who made the Mother of God the Son so "great." This is to say that in reciting the rosary we sing the praises of God, who made Her great. At the same time we meditate upon the many mysteries that declare Her greatness as well as His.

Jesus said Moses wrote of Him, and John tells us some of the Apostles met the man spoken of by Moses (John 1:45; 5:47).

Jesus had to be thinking of that "woman," the tree of life (Gen. 2:9), as we shall see later. And also was He thinking of Gen. 3:15 and the fulfillment of the major prophecy? When Jesus tells us we must eat His body and drink His blood (John 6:50-58) in order to have divine life, is He not speaking about His own human nature taken from Mary, whom Elizabeth praised when she said, "Blessed is the fruit of your womb"?

When Jesus goes further and explains that this "eating" is to be a sacramental eating—"it is the spirit that gives life; the flesh profits nothing"—is He not telling us what is written all over the New Testament Scriptures that we need the Spirit of Christ (which is divine)?

When Jesus (Yahweh) so commanded Parent and his wife "to so eat," was He not disclosing *what* Parent and his wife were to eat of and how, to use the very words of Genesis? Were not the words of Jesus spoken in John 6:28-59, referring to the (divine) Person (Christ) of the Trinity, who, as man, had not yet come into the world at Parent's time as the "fruit of Mary's womb"!

When Jesus said, "It is the spirit that gives life; the flesh [human nature] profits nothing," was this not to hold true for the Parent *before* the Fall as well as after the Fall! And since it is, then the tree of life must be Mary, His Mother. The spiritual fruit of that tree of life must be the same identical fruit as the spiritual fruit of Her womb!

When Yahweh commanded Parent and His wife to

eat of the fruit of the tree of life lest they die the death ("everlasting death" as Mark clarifies it—Mark 3:29—or mortal sin, as we say today), was He not commanding the same thing in Genesis as He does in John 6:28-58!

When Jesus commanded us to eat His living body, was He not commanding us to eat of the fruit of Mary's womb! When Jesus insisted on using the word "eating" in connection therewith, even though the Pharisees ridiculed Him for it (John 6:60-65), He was but keeping alive the same figure, or the same word "eating," that Moses used in Genesis in connection with (the fruit of) "the tree of life." How could Jesus (Yahweh) ever let that catastrophe recorded in Genesis, chapters 1-3, die? Especially is this so whenever He thought of His own loyal Blessed Mother, and ours, with all Her sufferings, anguish, and travail beneath the Cross! Should one say *whenever* He thought of His Mother? Or should one say *as He was always mindful* of His Blessed Mother!

When Jesus in John 15:5 says, "I am the vine, etc.," does this make Mary any the less His Mother! Or is this to say He is disowning His own Mother when He changes to another figure of comparison!

When Jesus speaks about the "fruit of the vine," is He not still retaining the same figure of speech of the botanical order *fruit, tree, life!*

Fruit of the vine; *fruit* of your womb; *fruit* of the tree of life!

When Jesus in John 6:51 promises that those who eat this "bread come down from heaven *may never die*," He is not promising immortality of body, but of soul, with its divine life. It is the same as Yahweh Elohim promised Parent and his wife and offspring, as recorded in Genesis anent the eating of the fruit of the tree of life.

While it is true that Parent and his wife *before* the Fall were destined to have immortality of body, this was not to be the effects of eating of the tree of life. This was an out-right gift that came with the gift of integrity, which was a preternatural gift. The holiness of soul (divine life) whereby Parent and his wife (Gen. 5:1) were made to the image approximating the likeness of God, which elevated him to the level or realm but not the equal of God, was a supernatural gift. It is such even today *after* the Fall for those who receive Baptism (John 6:27-59).

When Yahweh said, "You shall die the death," He was referring to the death of God's abiding presence, or life, within the soul, not alone to their bodies. Had they not sinned, no one knows how long they would have lived on earth.

Who puts the so-called myth in Genesis? Is it not they who so read it into the text because of their erudition gained from the pagans!

Satan inspired Gilgamesh *et al.* with its falsity. And what a prevarication or shuffling in the meanings of words he accomplished!

God, who inspired and revealed His truths while He concealed them from the unbeliever, said, "But now they are hidden from your eyes" (read Matt. 13:35; Luke 13:35).

How blessed are we that Jesus left His infallible teaching Church to keep us from being deceived by Satan! For the sins of the spirit (the devil) against the Holy Spirit will not be forgiven either in this life or in the life to come (my translation from the Greek, Matt. 12:31-32).

When Jesus, therefore, said, "No one comes to the Father but by me" (John 14:6), to use our way of understanding, is this not to say we must first be introduced to Jesus by His and our own Mother Mary?

Therefore, let us pray to Mary, Queen of Peace and Queen of the Holy Rosary.

Why do we pray to Mary? It ought to be pretty clear,

regardless of which texts we use, that to Mary was assigned the office of being the Mother of all, in temporal matters as well as in matters spiritual (John 19:26-27; Luke 2:4 ff.). It ought to be clear that to Mary was assigned the ugly task of gaining the victory over Serpent and his seed (Gen. 3:14-15). It ought to be real clear that Her hands were perpetually entwined with the hands of the Holy Spirit by reason of Her virginity (Luke 2:34 ff.).

It ought to be clear that to the Holy Spirit is attributed the work of sanctification. The combined hands of them should get the job done.

Anyone ought to know that both temporal and spiritual activities cannot always be separated in this life. These must be performed out of love for God in order to be meritorious for heaven. Truly one must be alive and eat before one can love God. For, to love is to live.

It ought to be clear that the most natural and instinctive thing is for a child to go first to its mother. God understands, for He so built human nature, and we are human— or are we?

It ought to be clear that the same Holy Spirit who accepted Her for His servant so wants Her to perform. How else could She be His servant from high heaven unless in shielding Her children in the battle with Serpent! She served Her Son in His Crucifixion. He assigned Her to the task of helping His brethren, you and me, who also are Her children if we will so claim Her. Just where is the problem if one has the right kind of faith? O ye of little faith!

What better appeal than to hail Her as our Mother? Mother always understands even if men do not. For God made a mother smarter than a man for that precise purpose.

May we recite Her beads over and over to gain the battle against the evil ones! Frequently reciting Her rosary as we meditate upon all of the mysteries is bound to increase our faith. This will pay dividends never dreamed of. It is our safest path to heaven.

The reader will please pardon a further word on "trees" at the risk of being repetitious.

Our Lord speaks of trees in Matthew 12:33. As present-day texts render this quote, whether Protestant or Catholic, the intended revelation seems to be lost at the expense of rhetoric. For example, today the texts have, "Either make the tree good and *its* fruit good or make the tree bad and *its* fruit bad." The much older versions, both Catholic and Protestant read, "Either make the tree good and *his* fruit good or make the tree evil and *his* fruit evil; for by the fruit is the tree known." The newer versions have used the word *bad* in place of the older word *evil* in order to make the words come out more rhetorical. Such license is hardly permissible. However, one or other of the older Protestant versions has a footnote saying that perhaps the Latin word *eius* might be either "his" or "its," thus indicating they are not sure.

A careful reading of what Matthew writes previously in said chapter gives every indication that our Lord is referring to persons, more especially to the person of the devil, as well as to Himself.

To be sure, if the Lord is speaking about physical trees, then the Latin word *eius* should come translated as "its." But since He is speaking about trees as a person, then it must refer to said person as only "his" (*eius*). This is true because only persons are capable of good and/or evil morals—not trees.

Besides, good and evil are in contrast. Why bring in the words good and bad? The word *eius* must refer to "him" and not to "it."

Who is the person? The one with the good fruit would be God, as Augustine says. The person with evil fruit would be the devil. Or, as we have been using the expression, God, because of His abiding presence (grace), and the devil with his abiding presence, who brings forth his evil fruit, because of his pride, envy, and hate.

May we pray always to Mary, who is one with God, that His abiding fruit will be in and with us! Shades of the "tree of life"—Mary, our Life!

Gentle reader, if you think the greatness of Mary has been overestimated, then it is high time that you prayed to Her who is your Mother and the Mother of all mankind, for a fuller appreciation of Her greatness, as She so humbly said, "He that is mighty has made me great." Such a one needs a shock treatment. May this suffice. Words cannot begin to describe Her greatness, nor is the human mind of any genius able to comprehend Her greatness, much less able to give it proper expression.

If anyone thinks She has had a build-up equivalent to that of God, then such a one has but a very meager notion of God and His greatness. "Holiness is his name," She said. That is to say, He is the very quintessence of perfection and holiness.

Read something about the billions of light-years certain stars are from the earth, and this will give you a faint idea of the distance God is above Mary, who is "nature's solitary boast"; and the distance the sun is from the earth, and you will have an incomplete idea of how far we poor mortals struggling with the effects of original sin are from Her.

Pray that the Jewish people who disowned Her Son, as well as Her, who are of their own, may come to receive Him through Her intercession. Then we shall have peace on earth. Not that such are responsible for war and all the ills on earth. But as John said, "The synagogue of Satan" is (Rev. 2:9; 3:9). Why not pray to Mary in order to save America as well as to save our own immortal souls? For indeed She is the Mother of all mankind, the same as is Her Son the Redeemer of all mankind. We all know what a mother can and will do.

CHAPTER 12

Queen of the Rosary—
Mediatrix of Peace

Job wrote, "Life is a warfare." At the close of his gospel, Moses informs us that the first Eve mediated this warfare. For this state, Moses gave *hope* by promising the second Eve, who would mediate peace—Mary, our *hope* (Gen. 3:15). Job has quite a warfare portrayal with Satan. The latest: "Job is a myth." For some Job may be fiction, but Satan is no myth.

Moses accentuates the victory which the Lady will gain through Her Son over the evil, envious, hateful one, the spirit of evil, who is responsible for man's chaotic state. It marks the spiritual demise of all those who, either *in re* or *in spe,* refuse, because of a bad will, to hail Yahweh and His Lady as their King and Queen of Heaven and Earth: those who refuse Operation Holy Spirit through the Mediatrix of Peace (Acts 7:51).

By the expression *in re* is meant all those in "the Master's house" who actually and really "eat at the Master's table," while those *in spe* are such as "eat of the crumbs that fall from their masters' table," and have a good will (Matt. 15:27). These latter are not really and actually members of the Master's family. Because of ignorance and their good will, these are "related" to the family of the Master, as Pius XII points out (cf. Mystic Body). Of these latter it might be asked, "Will such get to heaven? They may, but they cannot be sure without the certitude that comes from faith wrought through the infallibility of the Church.

Moses' major prophecy makes those other words come to life, also spoken with a spirit of prophecy, and quoted by Christ to "the children of the devil," as He called those with a bad will: "The Lord said in prophecy to my Lord: 'Sit on my right hand until I make thine enemies thy footstool' " (Matt. 22:44).

God never forgot what Serpent did to His original plan for His queen, and what Serpent brought on Her because of the alternate plan—She, the Queen of Martyrs.

The original idea *of* His coming was never changed. But the plan *for* their coming had to be changed, in the meantime, from one of joy and glory to that of a "Man of Sorrows" with "His Queen of Sorrows." In *joy* and *glory* they will not come until the end of time (Matt. 24:30, 25:31; Luke 9:26; 21:27; Apoc. 19:16; John 16:20).

Since footstools are for comfort and relaxation, by way of foot rests, we see now why God the Father represents God the Son at ease with His feet resting upon the mounded lid of earth's remains: those who have everlasting envy and hatred for the King and the Queen. In an extended sense of the metaphor, the damned devils, and their own, shall burnish the "heel" (foot) of the King and the Queen forever, in darkness. Let Paul describe it: ". . . and what is the exceeding greatness of his power and majesty towards us, who believe according to the might of his power, which he wrought in Christ, raising him up from the dead, and setting him on his right hand in the heavenly places. Above all principalities, and power, and virtue and dominion, and every name that is named, not only in this world, but also in that which is to come. And he hath subjected all things under his feet, and hath made him head over all the Church, which is his [social] body, and the fulness of him who is filled all in all." (Eph. 1:19-23.)

God says, "I hate a mouth with a double tongue" (Prov.

8:13). Serpent had, and still has, a double tongue. He is skilled at shuffling the meaning put to words, as we have seen; always set to the purpose of deceiving or "seducing." If his words were money, men would not be so slow in detecting which is counterfeit. His house of business is on the street that leads to that "little city" where matters of faith and morals are always on display at a price. His gain is to present the false imitation of the true. His most successful appeal is that of liberty: "Your eyes will be opened." It is eye (sense) appeal, not mind appeal. Witness how the world is falling for Communism, even here in the U.S.A. A Protestant bishop said, "If it is going to be Catholicism or Communism, then give us Communism." A student of his, before he became a bishop, informed me they no longer prayed, but substituted sociology for theology.

The best and safest mind appeal is that of divine-faith appeal, which is as strong as God's mind. Satan keeps the price of faith in himself marked "low cost" and points to the "high cost" of faith in God. But he never tells his customers that he is bargaining for perdition, and that heaven cannot come at too great a cost; and that one gets what one pays for; or that Christ purchased us at a great price, the price of His own most precious blood (I Cor. 6:20; 7:23; I Pet. 1:18), as His Mother, Mary, paid the price too.

It is the purpose of metaphor to elevate the mind by way of suggestion to truth that is both inspiring and revealing. The prophecy of God—major prophecy indeed—found in Genesis 3:14-15 is the climax to the gospel of Moses. The gospel of Moses gives the spiritual genesis of the soul of mankind, from the start, with Parent. When Moses wrote, there was naught that could have been done to better the state of things for mankind in Parent. But what could bring great comfort and *hope* to mankind after the Fall, and at the time of Moses' writing, he, Moses puts in the major prophecy which projects the new nature of the new spiritual genesis of mankind unto the end.

This is done in metaphor that conceals from the apostate and the disbeliever and the pagan the glories of the revelations of God, while the believer regains the promise of a better *hope* (Rom. 5:2; 8:20; Eph. 2:12; Col. 1:20; Tit. 2:13). "For God created man immortal; and to his own personal image he made him. But by the envy of the devil, death came into the world [of man and angel], and they follow him who are of his side" (Wisd. 2:23-24, Greek reading).

Mary not only was *of* God's side; She was always *at* His side. She now, body and soul, "sits" at His side for all eternity (Heb. 4:10-11). And those here below who are *of* Her side, because they are with Christ, and against Serpent, shall be with Him *at* Her side in heaven.

Perhaps it would be sharper to say with Stephen, the first martyr, that Mary rather *stands* now, than sits, until She will have tucked all Her children safely in Paradise, thus to bring out Her anxious powers of intercession (cf. Acts 7:55), to use a mother's way of thinking and speaking and doing.

When God uttered the famous prophecy, recorded for us by Moses, which promised that Serpent's continued hatred, born of envy against the Lady, should never die, He implicitly revealed all that we have come to know of Her by later and more explicit revelations in His New Testament religion. Moses, as a matter of fact, announced that the battle would be between Serpent and the Lady; between Serpent's followers and Her followers (Hebrew reading only).

This all-important prophecy synthesizes in its meager embrace the entire history of life among men to come upon earth unto the end. The battle lines are announced therein as having been tightly drawn for the ensuing series of conflicts.

It should be stated as a philosophical axiom that whatever is created is, by that fact alone, imperfect. The created
human person, or angelic person, is imperfect for the simple
reason that there is required, from the outset, if either is to
exist, the Supreme Person of God to create them. Since these
persons need to be created if they are to exist, they also require a continued presence of the genius of the Creator to
keep them created. This is a terrific imperfection in the
creature. This imperfection is so great that it equates itself
with nothingness in the first and last analysis and contrasts
the created with the Creator, who is everything. (1 Tim. 6:7;
Gal. 6:3.)

Only God the Creator, who is the uncreated, has the perfection which requires no genius of creation, because He always IS. He always is uncreated and for that reason is called
holy, or, better, Holiness, which is perfection. Such perfection
which is God is terrifying. It equates itself in the mind of
one who has thought it through with the expression "One is
in awe of Him"; that is, one has a reverential fear of Him;
one is ever grateful to Him; one cannot help but love Him
for giving one existence; one is truly repentant in His presence. These equations come bound in one word, *worship*. If
giving honor to men is standard for mankind, why not "worship," which God demands! We worship God *privately* by
believing all that He has revealed and makes known through
His infallible Church. We worship Him publicly by offering
the sacrament of His true and real body in each: the bread
and the wine of the Mass.

No people boast more about their own culture than do
we Americans. We are always bragging about our wealth and
power.

Little do we realize that the very word *culture* is bound
up with the word *worship,* which means to honor a people

for the greatness of the development of their natural resources.

For some time now we have been hanging our heads due to our low culture.

Human perfection of the highest kind is civilization, or culture, which calls for unity in fundamentals.

We must first recognize our faults, then admit them, as Paul VI did publicly, then begin to improve our personal dignity—true freedom in the privacy of our lives—by using well our gifts and the values of life, plus God's grace in achieving excellence.

What human person is more excellent than Mary? May She be our mediator and model. Truly is She our very hope!

If one will use his reasoning powers, correctly "mixed with faith," he will soon see that the very existence of God, strictly speaking, cannot be proved, as one's own existence cannot be proved. One's own existence is a truth that is co-natural to one's own mind. God's existence too is co-natural to human intelligence. It might be said, in passing, that one can only demonstrate his own existence; he also can demonstrate, but only demonstrate, the existence of God—not prove it. A person who is honorably intelligent requires no proof of his own existence; neither does he require proof of the existence of God. As stated above, he recognizes either as a truth already known (Rom. 1:20).

However, since one is imperfect, which imperfection is attested to by the mere fact that one has not always had existence and therefore, has been created, one must be most careful lest he contravene the two things by the knowledge of which is co-natural to him. That is to say, he must be on his guard lest the co-natural idea of God's existence become so notably forgotten while he plays up the co-natural idea of his own existence that the two co-natural ideas merge, as it were, into one. If this happens, then the individual will begin to think that he himself is God. The truth of the matter is that when one becomes an atheist or agnostic, that one has allowed his ego to come between himself and God. He has forgotten God. Such a one becomes his own god. He requires no religion, he thinks, because he exercises no relation with anyone but himself. The sun rises and sets on himself. He finds himself with no relations with God, which religion is; he has no religion other than self-exaltation. To himself he becomes self-existent; a law unto himself alone; answerable to no one. Today it is known as existentialism—false, of course.

God foreknew this, so He equipped both angel and man at the outset of their beginning with superadded gifts, both created and uncreated, whereby they might keep sharply outlined their relations with God and worship Him, their sole benefactor.

But Satan's ego came between himself and God. Satan became his own god. He bargained for the worshipful services of other angels, and obtained them. Now Satan bargains for men, but by telling men there is neither God nor devil, neither heaven nor hell. The ordeal whereby Lucifer became his own god is termed, in child language, pride. It brooks the presence of no other god, real or imaginary. The true God is thus outlawed.

This pride does not destroy the existence of the true God as a reality, but it does tend to make of Him a mock reality which is the birth of envy, followed by hatred.

The glory of the tree of life and the glory of the fruit of the tree of life and all her children automatically become objects of scorn, envy, and hatred.

This explains why Moses wrote "and all their array." Angel and man were prepared by God with suitable endowments to thwart any insubordination from within their very selves in the first place, and from such as might come from without themselves. When Moses writes that the "hatred will continue," he is telling us in the first place that the Lady, His Mother, will come adorned with all the glory God can adorn Her with. He is telling us that Her family too shall come into the possession of these adornments in order that they may merit heaven, the very purpose "of their existence." He is telling us that there shall be wars and battles all engendered by Satan, who hates the Virign Lady and those associated with Her. This explains why the Church is always the target of persecution. No, Catholics have not a persecution complex, but are prepared for a persecution simplex.

This should make it evident to anyone that to say that the "woman" in this prophecy refers to Eve is proximate to heresy. Certainly Adam's wife was nothing to be envious of, after the Fall. However, insofar as Adam's wife, by the grace of God, returned to the state of grace as a child of God, she would have been an object of envy on Satan's part.

But Eve as an individual represented no one. She had no official capacity. Moses is now writing of a far, far greater triumph than anything the impotent wife of Adam could ever accomplish.

When the promised Lady came from her mother Ann, she was called Mary. Mary always meant "lady," also "peace." Later She was called Eden by the angel, that is, "full of grace." When She accepted that epithet, come from heaven, She said, "Henceforth all my children shall call me Eden: full of grace [blessed]" (Greek reading). The first of Her children to call Her "blessed" was the angel Gabriel: "Blessed art thou among women" (Luke 1:28). Gabriel might as well have called Her Queen of the Angels. Originally Lucifer refused to so honor Her, and he still does.

BRIGHT: While I appreciate more than words can tell the immensity and depth of your lengthy explanation on the

Queen of the Rosary, Mediatrix of Peace, would you mind going into detail concerning the genesis of the New Man and also give further dimension to the infallibility of the Pope?

FATHER: Mr. Bright, nothing would suit me better, if you will have the patience to hear me out at great length.

CHAPTER 13

The Genesis of the New Man: Part A

If one is to believe the revelations of the Scriptures (and who will deny them?), there is an error spread at large that will need to be overcome if men are to be converted not only to the teachings of Christ but to Christ himself. There ever have been, and there are today, those who think or suppose their own native genius can confer upon them the light of understanding of God's truth, and that the warmth of their own human wills can make them wax strong in His love. Nothing is further from the truth. There are others who feel the brilliance of their favorite human author, or some eloquent orator—or they may attribute it even to the Bible itself —can furnish them all the light they need for conversion. It is quite a mistake, and argues surely to the conclusion that such persons have not captured the revelation concerning the absolute importance of the supernatural. You will hear another say, "So-and-So converted me"; that too is a mistake. Every conversion to God is of God, by God, and in God, and through God or because of God.

It matters not how brilliantly one may set forth the teachings of Christ about the supernatural. It is still by that token no more than a human representation, or natural presentation, of learning about the divine truth. Whether it be divine truth Himself, or any of His revealed truths, such cannot be accepted as supernatural by any person until the grace of God has laid hold of him and given him the divine understanding about the divine truth. Let the gospel narrative carry the argument.

The Divine Author makes the Evaneglist write the answer to the above problem in no unmixed terms: "This man came to bear witness concerning the light. . . . He [John] is not the person called the light. He is [only] to bear witness that all men might believe through *him* [the Light] because he is the light, the true light, which enlightens every man that comes into the world." What could be clearer than the foregoing words? A greater, a holier prophet than John the Baptist never lived, and yet despite his preachings, says the Divine Author, he could not furnish the light for believing and converting. The light had to come through Christ in the Holy Spirit. Indeed, the Author says, "Grace and truth came through Jesus Christ" (John 1:17), and not from the Baptist. "No man hath seen God at any time: the only begotten Son who is in the bosom of the Father, he hath revealed him" (John 1:18).

One of the most beautiful stories of the Lord's sojourn on earth is told by Luke (19:1 ff.). This story is used here in an accommodated sense.

A certain man by the name of Zacheus, who was a runt in stature but a rich man, and therefore, we suppose, smart, heard that the Christ was passing by. "He sought to see Jesus, who he was. So he climbed up in a sycamore tree." The record does not go on to tell us that Zacheus saw Jesus, and who He was. On the contrary, it states that Jesus, looking up, saw Zacheus and told him to come down. "Zacheus, make haste and come down; for this day I must abide in thy house." And he made haste and came down; and received him with joy . . . and Jesus said to him. "This day is salvation come to this house, because he also is a son of Abraham." Is Jesus referring to the house of his domesticity or to the "temple" of his own soul as He did on that occasion when the Pharisees thought He meant otherwise? (I refer to that occasion when they thought "his temple" referred to the Temple of Jerusalem).

Of course, the first impulse is to give a restricted narrow, natural interpretation to these words, whereas all Scripture is susceptible of a spiritual or supernatural meaning. To the unbeliever, without the eyes of faith, such a one sees in the word *house* no more than the publican's (tax gatherer's) residence (physical) into which our Lord entered. Even the people so reacted according to the record, on the occasion: "And when all saw it, they murmured, saying, that he was gone to be a guest with a man that was a sinner."

But what did Jesus reveal for us on this occasion? He made it known that while the sycamore tree did furnish a vantage point of place for physical seeing with "the eyes of flesh and blood," it took the eyes of faith and the light that Jesus gave Zacheus when He "looked up at him" to make it possible for Zacheus to "receive him into his *house* with joy." Jesus "knocked at the gate" of his mortality, and Zacheus received Him. He believed and He loved. He was made. That there can be no doubt about this interpretation is evident from Hebrews 3:1-11. Paul there uses the word *house* in the sense of the person of a man individually, and also collectively as household or family (religion). But one scarce should grasp the supernatural meaning from the English versions without the aid of the Greek: "Every house is furnished by someone, but God is the furnisher of all [*ta panta*] houses": i.e., persons furnished with the wedding garment of sanctifying grace. Christ, however, is faithful as a Son over his own house. "We are that house [household, family], provided we persevere, etc." (Heb. 3:1-11.)

For He it is who said, "He that believeth in me . . . and loveth me, he will keep my word, and my Father will love him, and we will come to him, and will make our *abode* with him." Yes, the Father entered into the soul (house) of Zacheus, together with the Son and the Holy Spirit, and salvation came to the "house" of Zacheus, because he was a "son of

Zacheus, because he was a "son of Abraham." Why mention Abraham? Was this gentleman put in the state of salvation because he was a Jew? No, not if one understands the spiritual meaning which Jesus gives to his own words. The word *Abraham* is a Hebrew word that means "father of the multitude." Hence Zacheus now is in the state of salvation because through the Spirit of Christ he has become a child of God, the true father of the multitude, a thing which natural birth did not, and could not, confer upon him. God's love and life and light are uncreated, and must come down from the Father of lights. Zacheus became a member of the corporate religion family.

Zacheus announced to the Lord that he was, and had been, a man of prayer and penance, which are the two important forerunners for the grace of faith and conversion, which grace, or favor, theologians call prevenient grace.

Just to prove that this is no idle dream, let me quote to you from the Divine Author's other words which seal His meaning to His words: "Such as I love, I rebuke and chastise. Be zealous, therefore, and do penance. Behold, I stand at the gate, and knock. If any man shall hear my voice, and open to me the door, I will come in to him, and will sup with him, and he with me" (Rev. 3:19-20). Could words be more potent?

But what do they mean? Well, again let us turn to the Scriptures. Everyone is familiar with the furtive glance that Jesus gave Peter after the denial: "And the Lord turned and looked upon Peter [said not a word]. And Peter remembered the word of the Lord, as he had said: 'Before the cock crow thou shalt deny me thrice.' And Peter going out wept bitterly." (Luke 22:61.) Peter was converted. What brought about the conversion? Here we have the demonstration of Zacheus repeated, and the fulfillment or the dramatization of the Lord standing at the *gate* and knocking. No, the record does not say He stands at the *door,* as the artist pictures it. No, He is a better lover than that, or should I say wooer. Christ represents Himself as standing out at the *gate* on the street, on the outside, in the cold of earth's creation. God, who creates man and keeps him created, stands nigh unto what He has created. Paul in the Acts adumbrates this revelation beautifully:

"God, who made the world and all that is in it, since He is the Lord [Saviour] of the angels and of men (the heavens and the earth), does not dwell in temples built by hands; . . . And from one man He has created the whole human race and made them live all over the face of the earth, determining their appointed times and the boundaries of their lands; that they should seek God, and perhaps grope after him and find him, though he is not far from any one of us. For in him [the Father] we live, and in him [the Son] we move, and in him [the Holy Spirit] we have our being [Jesus owed His human being to the Holy Spirit], as indeed some of your own poets have said, 'For we are also his offspring.' If, therefore, we are the offspring of God, we ought not to imagine that the Divinity is like to gold or silver or stone, or to an image graven by human art and *thought.* The times of this ignorance God has, it is true, *overlooked,* but now he calls upon all men everywhere to repent; inasmuch as he has fixed a day on which he will judge the world with justice by a Man whom he has appointed, and whom he has guaranteed to all by raising him from the dead. Now when they heard of a resurrection of the dead, some began to sneer, but others said, 'We will hear thee again on this matter.' . . . Certain persons joined him and became believers." [Acts 17:24-34]

He casts a ray of light through the window of the soul which is the mind of the one whom He is striving to woo, and which, in the imagery, is "the gate" at which He knocks. If the light is effective, that is, if it is "absorbed," accepted, "lapped up" with interest, the next step is to hear His voice. "If today you hear his *voice,* harden not your hearts, etc." (Heb. 3:7). And what is His voice? God's teachings come to life with the light of His love. Then He is bidden, "Enter."

Peter had been warned, "Before the cock crow twice, thou shalt deny me thrice." He who lacked the will to believe those words now had those words come to life within him, with dramatic suddenness, and power of conversion. All of which proved, no matter how brilliant the teacher, if one does not use the accompanying grace, God's revelations will have no meaning, or at most will receive a natural, earthly meaning. We will still be "up the tree" but will be unable to see the Christ with the eyes of faith, and to love Him with His divine will of love. Need more be said! "Which of you by thinking can add to his stature one cubit" (Matt. 6:27), whether physical, moral or spiritual! Will we sneer or will we believe!

So while one rides upon the shoulders of an evangelist, even of the Baptist or the Scriptures, or stands upon the tiptoes of his own intellectual genius, or his own existentialism, he may be able to add a few inches of forensic supernal thinking to his imagined stature of existentialism, but it will not change the nature of the man, except for the worse. For such a one will not even have "his feet upon the ground"; nor will it afford him powers for divine understanding. Without the help of the supernatural life, he will not be big enough "to sup" with the Divine Guest in his "own house"; and crutches of intellectual pride will be of no spiritual advantage; rather, because of them he will fall.

From God's own words it becomes evident how foolish and how futile are the attempts on our part, no matter how learned we may be in other matters, or even in the written Word, to strive to save our own souls in our own way, that is, in preference to *His way.*

The abyss between the created and the uncreated is so infinite that we shall require His added stature of thinking and loving, which will mean believing and loving with His grace. Without it we shall remain members of the kingdom of darkness, the kingdom of Satan into which we were born by natural birth. Regardless of the amount of wishful thinking to the contrary, or emotionalism, and autosuggestion, the most one might change oneself will be into an imaginary angel of light (II Cor. 11:14) worthy of "the darkness outside" (Matt. 22:13).

It is important, therefore, to receive Him *personally* if His words are to come to life in us. "To as many as received him, to them he gave the power of *being made* the sons of God, to them that believe in his name" (John 1). This process "of being made" is one that freely begins and must continue on ever increasing levels until the sleep of death transfers one into the eternal nuptials: "This confidence we have in you, that he who hath begun a good work in you, will perfect it unto the day of Christ Jesus" (Phil. 1:6), "if so ye continue in the faith" (Col. 1:23).

Perseverance and patience are required: "Are you so foolish that whereas you began in the Spirit, you would now be *made perfect* by *nature?*" (Gal. 3:3). "Laying aside every weight of sin, let us run by *patience* to the fight [with the devil] . . . looking on Jesus, the author and finisher of faith" (Heb. 12:2). "Thou hast patience and hast endured [persevered] for my name, and hast not fainted" (Apoc. 2:3, 10, 19; 14:12).

Since there must be two beginnings in every man's life if he wishes to get to heaven, the one natural and the other supernatural, let us take up, with the Author of the supernatural, the spiritual genesis of man, in the study of His way.

The surety that God's heavenly light, or grace, is a pre-requisite that must be antecedent to and accompany every step of the rational creature in the process "of being made the sons of God" under Operation Holy Spirit, is guaranteed by Christ, in His response to the Pharisee Nicodemus (John 3:1 ff.).

Exactly what Nicodemus had in his question that pro-voked from Christ His mighty oath, the record does not state in words. If you will recall, in Chapter 2 above, mention was made that the frugal Hebrews did not always put the ques-tion into writing. That was to be inferred from the wording of the answer. Fortunately for us, Christ—the official author of this text—also gives the official implication of what the question might have been.

Throughout the gospel that bears John's name, Christ has been contrasting the kingdom of darkness and the kingdom of light; the kingdom of this world and the kingdom of God; the kingdom "beneath" and the kingdom "above." "And Jesus said to them, 'You are from *beneath,* I am from *above.* You are *of* this world. I am not of this world'" (John 8:23); "You are *of* your father the devil . . . I have not a devil" (John 8:44, 49). Jesus had no devil because He was sealed at the time of His incarnated conception by the Holy Spirit, the oil of gladness (Heb. 1:9). His birth from the Immaculate Virgin prevented the original sin from passing on to Him by way of generation, as it has to us.

To enter the kingdom, one must come by faith in His voice. "But his voice you do not see whence it originates," but you shall know that it is through the sacrament of faith. "For they shall all be taught of God." My Father will draw them "by his grace through his Spirit." (John 6:44-45, 66.) "My sheep hear my voice and they follow me" (John 10:27).

In order, therefore, that one may abandon "the kingdom

of darkness," which earthly birth brought him, for membership in the "kingdom of light"; leave the kingdom of death
for the kingdom of life; relinquish the kingdom of error for
the kingdom of truth; remain *in* the world, but not *of* the
world; be numbered no longer among those from "beneath"
but with those "born from above"; desert one's father, the
devil, in order to cry, "Abba"—"Father"—to God; walk out
on the bankruptcy of Satan's empty promises, in order to
become "heirs also, heirs indeed of God and joint heirs with
Christ" (Rom. 8:14-47); cease to be "by nature children of
wrath" in order to become, and to be made, His supernatural
children of grace; shed the livery of slaves, servants of Satan,
for the liberty-loving livery of the "wedding garment" of peace
with the heavenly bridegroom, etc., etc.: what shall be the
order of procedure?

Christ said: (1) To those who are dead: "I know, if thou
wilt ask of God, God will give it thee" (John 11:12).
(2) "Whatsoever you shall ask the Father in my name, that
I will do" (John 14:13). Therefore pray, "Our Father who
art in heaven" (Matt. 6:9). (3) "They shall all be taught
of God" (John 6:45). Therefore, look up for yourself a
Teacher who has the divine faith, and who believes with
supernatural faith, and divine understanding all of His revelations. Nothing less will do. For "the symposium of faith
cometh by hearing" (Rom. 10:17). Nicodemus, unlike the
centurion, did not believe that Christ's words meant what
they said (John 3:12).

"No man can come to me except the Father draw him"
by His grace (John 6:44). Therefore, you need not expect
the brilliance nor "the persuasive words of [human] wisdom"
(I Cor. 2:4) to do the converting; neither need you be afraid
(Rom. 10:11) of what is taught, because "the truth will set
you free" (John 8:32). It will be the simple, honorable matter of an exchange; the exchange of selfish functional freedom

for the liberty-loving freedom of Christ, "with the freedom wherewith he will make us free" (Gal. 4:31). Because "Now the Lord is a Spirit, and where the Spirit of the Lord is, there is liberty" (II Cor. 3:17). Surely no one will be worried about one's liberty when one is resting in the arms of God, who is love.

"Wherefore, as the Holy Spirit saith: Today, if you hear his voice, harden not your hearts . . . while it is today" (Heb. 3:8), for "the Holy Spirit breathes wheresoever he wills, and you hear his voice, but you do not see whence it [the voice] originates" (John 3:8), because "I stand at the gate and knock. If any man shall hear my voice, and open up to me the door, I will come in to him, and will sup with him, and he with me" (Rev. 3:30). "Amen, amen, I say unto thee: he that believeth in me hath everlasting life" (John 6:47). On the other hand, "If you will not believe, neither will you understand" (Isa. 7:9).

Therefore, one prays for the grace of the invisible Baptism in order to be able "to see the kingdom of God." With the aid of these flashes of light one will be enabled to find "the laver of regeneration and of renovation of the Holy Spirit . . . through Jesus Christ . . . that he may be an heir, according to the hope of life everlasting" (Tit. 3:5-7), "for without it, it is not possible to enter into the kingdom of God. That which is born of human nature is human earthly kind; and that which is born of the Holy Spirit, is the heavenly, godly kind. Do not wonder that I said to you: It is binding upon you to be born from *above*." (John 3:7-9.) Only the "waters" of God's grace can prevent the fires of hell.

This rebirth affair is required as of prime necessity because of what Papa and Mamma Adam accomplished by causing us all to be born into the state of original sin and deprived of God's abiding presence in our own "house."

By the strangest of all paradoxes, be it said that in order

for one to be and to be called a man, that one must be divine. Therefore, in order to be fully human one must be divine.

At this point there rises to the surface the reason for the title of this book. In Genesis 1:26, God proposed to Himself to make man (all of mankind, that is, *adam*) on the natural level with intelligence, etc., so he could in that capacity imitate God somewhat; and on the supernatural level, so that he might be an approximate likeness of God.

In 1:27, God set to work and so created the Parent (*ha adam*). Finally in 5:2 we are informed that after the created man and his wife had been so made (constituted) in the state of justice and holiness, only then was it that "he called *their* name man [adam]." Thus was it that the divinized man was entitled to be called "man," or as we say, to be acknowledged as "the whole man."

In this light, what becomes of Aristotle's "rational animal"? According to God's blueprint, a man must be much more than that. In order to qualify as a man one must be in the state of grace, otherwise he is a most incomplete man. And might one conclude from the Bible that such a one is not even entirely rational!

CHAPTER 14

The Genesis of the New Man: Part B

The most obvious thing about the obvious, oftentimes, is that it is not as obvious as it obviously should be. The obvious thing in all of revelation is that God created man for the express purpose of finishing and completing man through a free surrender and cooperation with God's supernatural genesis and sanctification. That can happen only in Operation Holy Spirit. God shares His nature and love with man. This, as has been said so often, cannot be created in man, or God would have created His love permanently in him. It is bound up with the mystery of divine love which includes these three.

Love is personal, selfless, and free. (1) It is personal. "Behold, *I* stand at the gate and knock." (2) It is selfless. "What greater love than this, that a man lay down his life for his friends?" (3) It is free. God, who is charity, or love, being Supreme Truth, must be supremely free. For love must reside in and flow from the will, which in turn, by its nature, follows the will. "Where the Spirit of the Lord is, there is freedom" (Cor. 3:17).

What greater love can there be than to possess and to be possessed of the Supreme Being? All this, of course, is of faith, as every courtship should be. But this courtship differs from the natural in this, that there can be no stealing of a march on the divine nuptials which are reserved for the unopened doors of heaven. That is why so much emphasis is put upon faith in the Scriptures and upon hope in what is to come. It is for this reason that normally we do not *experience* His abiding presence!

Since man comes into the world deprived of God's personal love, he naturally is full of self. In Baptism this new love starts with, and is designed to improve with, the corresponding measure of selflessness. "He that overcome shall thus be clothed in white garments" (Rev. 3:5; cf. 3:12, 21).

The Creator has implanted in everyone, even by creation, some kind of thirst or predilection for God. More often than not, this thirst or urge is expended upon some human idol because of its not being recognized or because of a faulty interpretation. But God wants a more elevated romance than nature affords, that is, one that is supernatural, personal, and spiritual. He desires to communicate everything for its success. Hence the Divine Author makes John quote Him in the use of terminology that is peculiar to love. We find the terms "adore," "thirst," "refresh," "the gift," "the water," "a fountain of water, springing up into life everlasting" (John 4:14).

But why the emphasis on "water" and kindred terms? (1) Christ is come a great teacher. He is strong for pictorial education, in order that man may come to approach the supernatural from the natural, but coupled with His grace. He tells us in this same chapter: "My meat is to do the will of him that sent me, that I may perfect his work" (John 4:34) . . . "the work which the Father hath given me to perfect" (John 5:36). And what is His work? His work is to *make* man, or the part of man in original sin, a whole man in "His likeness" and in "His holiness." Note these following texts.

"On the day God created man, He made him in his likeness" (Gen. 5:1). "And God completed on the sixth day the work [of divine art: Hebrew meaning] which He had made" (Gen. 2:2). But Parent was to *perfect* that work in the course of his own life upon earth.

"Is not he thy Father, because that he possessed thee, and because that he made thee" (Deut. 32:6. trans. from the Hebrew).

"Patience hath a perfect work, that you may be [made] perfect and entire" (James 1:4).

Paul said: The very purpose "of the ministry of Christ is that we may present every man perfect in Christ Jesus" (Col. 1:25-29); "furnished to every good work" (II Tim. 3:16-17); "looking on the author and finisher of faith" (Heb. 12:2); "being confident that he who *began* a good work in you will perfect it unto the day of Christ Jesus" (Phil. 1:6); in "the mystery which has been hidden from ages and generations" (Col. 1:26); "looking on Jesus the author and finisher of faith . . . in santification . . . and holiness . . . without which no man shall see God" (Heb. 12:2, 10, 14). The word *holiness* equates with the word *whole*. Both derive from the same root word. Such is God's blueprint.

But what will be the price? Let the Divine Author answer that through His great convert-writer Paul: "For whom God loveth, he chastiseth; and he scourgeth every son whom he receiveth. Persevere under discipline. God dealeth with you as with his sons; for what son is there, whom the father doth not correct? But if you be without chastisement, whereof all are made partakers, then you are bastards [illegitimate], and not sons." (Heb. 12:6-8.)

Strong words these! One who has not God dwelling in his soul to *make* him the Father's son is a "bastard" of Satan's illegitimate kingdom. He is an illegitimate son, a part man, an incomplete man; not a whole man according to the original blueprint for a man as God "called" him in Genesis 5:2.

Jesus speaks of "water" often, as do the entire Scriptures. In the natural life water is indispensable for living; so also is "the water" of God's grace indispensable for divine and everlasting living now and forever. If you will note, the supernatural is destined to flow all along the line with the natural. That is as it should be, because the supernatural has its very name for that reason: it is to add something from "above" to the natural. Jesus said to the woman at Jacob's well, "You are drawing water from *beneath;* I will give you the living water from *above,* if you ask me" (John 4:10 f). Today theologians call it supernatural, and for that very reason.

Jesus cried out, "If anyone thirsts, let him come to me and let him who believes in me drink." As the Scriptures say, "From his [God's] bosom rivers of living waters shall flow" (John 7:38).

Men have always had the axiom that water seeks its own level, not only physically but also metaphorically, that is, in the social sense.

The water flowing from the Father and the Son in the Holy Spirit "shall become a fountain of water" seeking its level as it floats and elevates the man made "new" to the spiritual social level, and "fellowship" with God for everlasting disembarkation with the Trinity in heaven.

"Fellowship" means literally "to have things in common," and such is the Greek word in the original language: "What fellowship hath light with darkness" (II Cor. 6:14) . . . "That we may have fellowship with the Father" . . . "and one with another" (I John 1:3, 7).

The saving of Noah and his family *from* the water *by* the water was but a sign or symbol to man that his spiritual salvation will be effected through "the water that I will give you" (John 4:13).

Accordingly, one finds mention made of seven "rivers" springing up from the "fountain of water" that Jesus promises. (See Isa. 12:3.) Each is set forth in one way or another, by way of comparison, with seven different uses for water. The Holy Spirit is called "water" because He operates in many different ways for the seven outstanding purposes of life. Accordingly, Jesus left seven signs which have come to be and are called sacraments because they will make a man holy, and holier still if and when used with faith (Apoc. 22:11).

1. Water cleanses so that one may be fit for society. The Holy Spirit will cleanse for membership in His kingdom. "The laver of water by the word of life" (Tit. 3:5). And this is the spirit of the sacrament of Baptism (John 3:1 ff.).

2. Water is a sealer against contamination from air. "He that confirmeth us with you in Christ [one religion family], and hath anointed us, is God: who also has sealed us, and given the pledge of the Spirit in our hearts—from the princes [devils] of the power of this air, of the spirits who work on the children of unbelief" (Eph. 2:2). And this is the Spirit of the sacrament of Confirmation. St Paul calls it "renovation by the Holy Spirit" (Tit. 3:50).

When Paul came to Ephesus he found certain disciples. And he said to them, "Have ye received the Holy Spirit since ye believed? But they said to him: We have not so much as heard whether there be a Holy Spirit. And he said: In what then were you baptized? And they said, In John's baptism. Then Paul said: John baptized with the baptism of penance, saying: That they should believe in him who was to come after him, that is to say, in Jesus. Having heard these things, they were baptized in the name of the Lord Jesus." (Acts 19:1-5.) That is to say, they were baptized in the name of the Father and of the Son and of the Holy Spirit—the Baptism that had Jesus' name upon it (cf. Matt. 28:19). When "Paul imposed his hands upon them, the Holy Spirit came upon them."

3. Water nourishes and quickens health, and growth and life. "It is the Holy spirit that quickeneth; the flesh profiteth nothing. The words I have spoken to you, are spirit and life" (John 6:46-64). This is the Spirit of the sacrament of Holy Communion. "Take ye and eat, this is my body" (Matt. 26:26; I Cor. 10:16).

4. Water is a great detergent for dirt, pursuant to a reconciliation between unreconcilable elements. "He hath placed

in us the word of reconciliation" (II Cor. 5:17-20). He hath given us the Spirit of confession (James 5:16) which reunites or reconciles the repentant sinner, after Baptism, with Christ (John 20:21-24; James 5:16), and the Church (Vat. II).

5. Water cools, refreshes, uplifts. "If any one is sick . . . the [Spirit] Lord shall raise him up" (James 5:14-15). This is the Spirit of the sacrament of the Last Anointing, which readies the soul if the sick one is conscious, for immediate entrance into heaven, if that person should then die.

6. Water is a peaceful instrument of navigation for floating and delivery of precious cargo. "Every high priest is ordained to offer [float] the gifts and sacrifices . . . from man to God" (Heb. 5:1; 8:3). The Spirit of the sacrament of the priesthood. Through it God is worshipped by Christ in His religion family.

7. Water is essential for the mystery of multiplying growth in plants, both for food and for reseeding. The Spirit of Christ is essential to Matrimony, and to the mystery that multiplies members for the body of Christ—that it be done in God. Because "we have not here a lasting city, but we seek one that is to come" (Eph. 5:24-32; Heb. 13:14). The Spirit of the sacrament of Matrimony.

From the foregoing it is evident how Christ has arranged for man to have the Spirit, the Water, the Gift, overflowing in every important phase of his life upon earth. It elevates man into the realm of divinity, where individually as well as collectively, or should we say socially, a genesis and spiritual evolution begins with "rebirth from above." It is destined to continue at every important stage of man's life for the perfecting, completing, and finishing of the man whom God wills to make whole with a guaranteed final resurrection. Little wonder He said, "He that shall drink the water that I will give him, shall not thirst forever" (John 4:13), "and I will raise him up on the last day" (John 6:55). "If thou didst know the gift of God, and who he is that saith to thee, Give me to drink, thou perhaps wouldst have asked of him, and he would have given thee living water" (John 4:10). The woman was drawing water from below. Jesus would give the water from above: "But the water that I will give him, shall become in him a fountain of water, springing up into life everlasting" (John 10:14).

In the natural order, life requires drink and food. In living the supernatural life in the Spirit, "drink and food" also are required. Hence Christ shifts the imagery of comparison from "drink" to "eating": "He that cometh to me [through faith] shall not hunger and he that believeth in me shall never thirst" (John 6:35).

Seven times in the short space of a few texts Christ charges that "my flesh is meat" and that "unless you eat my flesh you will not have life in you. But if you eat my flesh, you will live in me as I live in the Father" (John 6:46-58). "Eating" is love language. The effect of eating is union. Love is personal union with God. Jesus also said, "My food [meat] is to do the will of him who sent me" (John 4:34; cf. John 4:8-34).

As usual, the disbeliever, the man without faith, says: "How can this man give us his flesh to eat" (John 6:53). The rationalist of this type immediately begins to think in terms of sense reactions. As such, the message of "eating his flesh" would become "a hard saying," aye, nauseating and revolting. But if one stops to realize he is in the presence of God speaking, and in the realm of the supernatural, he will, as he looks through the eyes of faith, hope, and love, find a supernal thing of ineffable proportions.

One must believe that Christ, God, who took bread and said, "Take, eat, this is my body," meant exactly what He said (Matt. 26:26). No, He did not say, "This bread is my body," but, "*This* is my body." Only one thing could have happened to the bread. What one thing could have happened?

Well, since the appearances of bread were still present in what the Apostles ate, and since Jesus said, *"This* is my body," there is but one alternative remaining. At His word the substance of the bread must have changed into the substance of His body, with accidents, or appearances, of bread remaining. This is transubstantiation.

To most persons the philosophic distinction, which is a real one, between substance and accidents is something new to their conscious thinking, albeit in their daily chatter, they make the distinction without being conscious of it. They speak of a man having an accident, a broken leg. The *man* was not broken (that is, his substance), but a lesser thing, an "accident," has hapened to his outward appearance, to his ability to walk. In the case of the bread, the opposite happened. Here it is hoped that the analogy of the accident of the broken leg will not be pushed so far that we get involved in semantics.

The thing that happened to the bread, because of the impact of Christ's commanding word power, was not that the outward appearance of the bread, that is, the accidents of the bread, were changed in any way whatsoever, but that the inward appearance of the bread, the substance of the bread, the substance which, not the eye of the body sees but the eye of the mind sees, was affected. Yes, it was so substantially affected that it was changed completely as to substance. How complete was the change? It was so complete that Christ no longer called it bread. He said, *"This* is my body," and that is how complete the change became. That is to say, the substance of the bread was changed into the reality of His body.

You should know that the substance of anything, even of the paper of this page, is not seen with the eye of the body but with the eye of the mind. From the sum total, ideas garnered through the five senses: seeing, tasting, touching, etc., the mind "sees" what this thing is, and calls it paper. Only the mind "sees" the substance of a thing.

The same must apply to His words: "I am the bread of life. . . . I am the living bread come down from heaven . . . and the bread that I will give is my flesh for the life of the world" (John 6:48, 51-52).

When Jesus says, *"This* is my body," I believe Him, because He says what He means, and He means what He says. Accordingly, with the new mind of faith, I see the substance of His body present, and reason tells me the substance of the bread can no longer be there, once God has so spoken. Why? Because I have a new set of appearances striking my elevated mind: not as to the bread, but because of the One speaking. I see and I hear that it is Christ who speaks, therefore I believe; and now I perceive with the mind of faith the Real Presence of the living flesh of Christ. I hear Jesus say, "This is my body" through the voice of the Church. What I hear the Church say, I believe. This is Catholic faith. I dare not dispute it nor doubt it.

Nevertheless, I still see with the eyes of my body the "trappings of bread" remaining. Do my senses, then, deceive me? My eyes, my touch, my taste are deceived, but not my hearing. No, it is not deceived, for I hear Jesus say, "This is my body" (Matt. 26:26). "Faith then comes by hearing; and hearing by the word of Christ" (Rom. 10:17). My natural mind yields to my "deeper" new mind—my elevated mind of faith. My new mind tells me it is His body. I now must believe and know it cannot be bread any longer. Jesus says so. Besides, one thing cannot be two things at the same time, nor can two things be one substantial thing.

But what happens to the substance of the bread? Does it cease to be? Was it annihilated? Only one thing could happen. It must be changed into the very substance of His living body with the accidents (appearance) of bread remaining. A little second-grader in my religion class once put it this way: "Jesus puts on clothes that look like bread."

And here let me advise that faith does not take reason away; on the contrary, it introduces reason into a higher field where it can work forever in striving to grapple with the subtleties which Christ and His faith present. Neither can one say any longer that faith is blind. It is the man who refuses to believe that remains blind—blind to the whole new panorama of truth on the supernatural level. Let me give you a sample of this, in this very "eating of His flesh" commandment.

Here we are in the throes of "love language" at its level lovely best. For God, who is love, is at the helm. He is no longer out on the street in the cold of creation, "knocking at the gate" to gain entrance. Once He has gained admittance through the door of faith and Baptism, He says, "If you Love me, you will want to eat me up." The believer says, "I love You, and I want to eat You up." Such is the language of lovers, not excluding the child for its mother and father; and He knew it. What did He do?

1. He found a way in which we can "eat Him up"—those of us who love Him, because of the contact through His faith.

He changes simple bread into the substance of His living resurrected body, having the accidents of bread remaining, so that one's natural senses at no time are nauseated from the "eating," and so that on our part, the challenge to faith becomes supremely rewarding. If we believe He is present because He says He is, and when the senses cannot see Him, then He knows, and we know, we are on the highest level of love's exchange in this vale of tears.

Love believes! Love is a Person! He is not present because we believe it. We believe in His Real Presence because we believe and know such is true after He or His priest speaks the words "This is my body and this is my blood."

2. The word *eating* is sometimes suggestive of chewing and digesting. But here the emphasis is not on the eating so much as on the effect of the eating, or union. The essence

of eating is swallowing, not chewing. Hence we swallow "the consecrated Host," and at that moment the Spirit of Christ pours forth into the soul to effect the communion (union) of our souls or spirits with the Spirit of supreme love: "As I live by the Father, so he that eateth me, the same shall live by me" and enjoy "the abundant life" (John 6:58; 10:10). This love life is personal.

What happens to the flesh, or the body, of Jesus? He tells us in John (6:64), "It is the spirit that gives life; the flesh profits nothing." Or, as the Greek allows the translation, "The flesh is wasted."

This is to say: So long as the Host (wafer) has the appearance of bread, Jesus is present with His living body, even in the stomach. When He loses His "clothes of bread," He disappears bodily, i.e., He ceases to be present, but His Spirit remains in the soul. This answers the unbelievers of Nicodemus' ilk who said, "It is unthinkable that Jesus' body should, by digestion, become excrement, wherefore I cannot believe in the Real Presence." Faith depends on hearing, and hearing upon the word of Christ (Rom. 10:17). I have His word for it. I dare not doubt or disbelieve. True, mysteries— many, to be sure—appear, but then, is not Jesus a great mystery! When Christ ceases to be present as soon as the "clothes of bread" are not sensible to the senses, then some other substance must come in that wake. Does this explain why various holy persons who were daily communicants lived without any other food whatsoever?

This is indeed the greatest love courtship ever indulged by man. It is designed to build us up, elevate us, to the supernal stage of perfection for the beatific vision when we shall be known even as we are known (I Cor. 13:13). He who creates in order to make is here fulfilling His eternal purpose, if we will welcome Him.

He once said, "A body thou hast fitted me" (Heb. 10:5),

in order that He might become incarnate. And so God wrapped the divine nature of His Son in flesh in Mary's womb that He might be born incarnate. Mary wrapped His body in the seamless robe in order that He might appear among men. The Father willed that by Jesus' agony, scourging, and Crucifixion, His Son be in the royal garments of His own blood in order that He might become king by conquest.

Now He wraps His flesh in the vesture of bread so that those whom He has made one religion-family by conquest into the seamless robe of His reunited kingdom might love and be loved by Him personally, and thereby have a guarantee of salvation (John 6:55). It is not a fleshly eating, but a spiritual eating. How suggestive it was that He be born in the "house of bread," the Hebrew meaning of Bethlehem! This eating today is called Holy Communion. This communicating with Him by all gives all the spirit of communicating with Him and also with each other, in the spirit of love.

"The Spirit is the life maker; the flesh profiteth nothing. The words I have spoken to you, *for which you ridiculed me,* they are Spirit, and they are life" (John 6:63, my own translation from the Greek).

Accordingly, "Jesus took bread, and blessed it, and broke it, and gave it to the disciples, and said, Take, eat; this is my body" (Matt. 26:26). In these words Jesus fulfilled His promise made in John, chapter 6, to give the banquet of His love for those who love Him so much that they will desire "to eat him up."

The believer says that Jesus, while He picked up bread from the table, gave not bread to them to eat, but His body. The unbeliever says, "I can't see it. How can bread become His body?" It never occurs to him that Jesus is God, and that He means what He says and says what He means. One might just as well ask, "How can He make us His sons?" However, the believer never says, "How?" to God. He believes, and waits for His understanding. After all, what difficulty is there for God, who gave bread its original substance, to change its substance into the new substance of His living body? And He who gives things their outward appearances—what difficulty is there for Him to substitute some other appearance: the appearance of bread in place of the appearance of His living body!

While the lengthy discourse of Jesus has much to say about "eating," the emphasis is to be placed not upon eating but upon the effect of eating, which is union with the Trinity of persons through the Spirit of Christ (cf. John 6:1-to end).

Behold the food, the bread of life, for the man whom God makes. And if you eat *not* this bread of life, you shall *not* have life in you. (John 6:54.) Thus spoke our Lord under oath, just to show He was declaring clear, literal revelation.

In order that anyone may be able to believe this great mystery of His divine presence under the appearance of bread, he will have to pray for the light of faith. "Therefore did I say to you, that no man can come to me, unless he has received the gift [of faith] from the Father" (John 6:66). If I can believe one thing that Jesus revealed, then I can believe all (catholic) that He has revealed, because, the credibility is the same, which is His infallible voice, the Church.

But why is it that men do not receive the Gift from the Father? Jesus answered this one: "Because men loved the darkness rather than the light: for their works were evil. For everyone that doth evil hateth the light, and cometh not to the light that his works may not be reproved" (John 3:20-21). "Blessed are the clean of heart, for they shall see God," even in this "bread" (Matt. 5:8).

True enough, men never do evil under the guise of evil. Rather, one is inclined to disguise error as truth and so deceive himself into thinking that he is *not* doing evil, but is doing good. But in the foreoging texts Christ tore the mask from such conduct. Such persons prate about their freedom and liberty, seemingly forgetting that truth governs liberty, as He said: "If you *continue* in my word you shall know the truth, and the truth shall make you *free*" (John 8:31-32)— that is, if you persevere in faith, in the truth. And Jesus said, "I am the truth." How does one continue in His word? By believing and doing His word.

Here it is interesting to note the nuance of meaning derived from Isaias 7:9 by the various translators apropos "believing." The Septuagint reading has: "If you believe not, you shall not understand." The King James: "If ye will not believe, surely ye shall not be established." And the Douay: "If you believe not, you shall not continue." The French has, "You shall not persevere."

The basic idea is one of love. The essence of successful lovers is to believe in each other. If love is to persevere, continue, perdure, there must be faith, founded on truth, which is the element of forming that oneness which is love. The Hebrew word means belongingness: two in one. On the human level two lovers must believe in each other if there is to be understanding, perseverance, one-ness. So also with our Lord.

In these, His following words, observe how Jesus blasts false freedom: "We have never been slaves to any man: how sayest thou, You shall be free? Jesus answered them: Amen, amen, I say unto you: that whosoever committeth sin, is the servant of sin. Now the servant abideth not in the house forever; but the Son abideth forever. If, therefore, the Son shall make you free, you shall be free indeed." (John 8:33-36.)

To those who abuse freedom by disguising error under the label of truth, while at the same time pleading ignorance, hoping such mental trickery will place them in the so-called category of those in "good faith," but yet forgivably ignorant, Christ has this real eye opener: "For judgment I came into this world; that they who see not, may see; and they who see, may become blind. And some of the Pharisees . . . said: Are we blind? Jesus said to them: If you were blind you should not have sin: ignorance excuses: but now you say: We see. Your sin remaineth. Your ignorance does not excuse. You are in bad faith." (John 9:39-41.) You had the light, but you spurned it. You have a bad will. Peace, grace, comes to those of good will: love.

Some there are who maintain that one should go easy on the teaching of Christ's truth, lest others be put in bad faith. Surely the above words should indicate the contrary. If it takes the grace of God to put one in the light in order to see and have good faith, then surely the same grace of God must be present to those who reject His teachings, which puts them in bad faith. Diplomacy, therefore, is not the *positive* element necessary for conversion. Rather is it the grace of God; for "all things are made through him, and without him is there not made anything of the things that are made" among rational personal creatures.

God created man in order to make mankind the Bride for His divine romance. Isaias says it all in one word: "For your Maker is your husband. The Lord of hosts is his name" (Isa. 54:5; Rev. 21:2). The religion-family is His bride: "Come and I will show thee the bride, the wife of the Lamb" (of God) who won His bride by conquest with His blood (Rev. 21:9).

From what we have learned thus far, among other things, this too is certain. The man that does not work his works under the influence of the grace of God is certainly not performing the works of God. No matter how right one's deeds are, if they are no more than what is called natural virtues, they are not of the supernatural vintage, and as such shall not be recorded in the Book of Life. God wants "godly deeds," deeds that are forthcoming from us as His adopted sons; those whom He makes by sharing His divine nature with them (II Pet. 1:4; cf. Denz. 190; II Cor. 3:4). Wherefore "I said you are gods" (Ps. 81:6; John 10:34), you "that receive the adoption of sons" (Gal. 4:4,6; Rom. 8:15:23 ff.). "Without me you can make nothing. Do the truth in love" (Eph. 4:15; II Cor. 10:31).

Since the Father and the Son and the Holy Spirit dwell within the soul that is in grace, because the Father and the Son communicate the Spirit to the soul, might we give at length a summary on the Trinity, one afforded by the "voice" of Christ:

That divine office which Jesus Christ received from His Father for the welfare of mankind, and most perfectly fulfilled, had for its final object to put men in possession of the eternal glory, and proximately during the course of ages to secure to them the life of divine grace, which is destined eventually to blossom into the life of heaven. Wherefore our Savior never ceases to invite, with infinite affection, all men, every race and tongue, into the bosom of His kingdom: "Come ye all to me, I am the life," "I am the good shepherd." Nevertheless, according to His inscrutable counsels He did not will to *entirely complete* and *finish* this office Himself on earth, but as He had received it from the Father, so He transmitted it for its *completion* to the Holy Spirit. It is consoling to recall those assurances which Christ gave to the body of His disciples a little before He left the earth: "It is expedient to you that I go, for if I go not, the Paraclete [helper] will not come to you: but if I go, I will send Him to you" (John 16:7). In these words He gave the chief reason of His departure and His return to the Father, the advantage which most certainly would accrue to His followers from the coming of the Holy Spirit, and at the same time He made it clear that the Holy Spirit is equally sent by, and therefore proceeds from, Himself as the Father; that He would *complete*, in His office of intercessor, consoler, and teacher, the work which Christ himself had begun in His mortal life. "My Father worketh until now, and I work" (John 5:17). For in the redemption of the world, and *completion* of the work, was by Divine Providence reserved to the manifold power of that Spirit who, in the creation, "adorned the heavens [that is, the angels]" (Job 26:13), and "filled the whole world [i.e, all rational creatures who surrender to Him]" (Wis. 1:7).

The mystery of the Blessed Trinity is the very "substance of the New Testament," that is to say, the greatest of all mysteries, since it is the fountain and origin of them all. In order to know and contemplate this mystery, the angels were created and sanctified above, and men upon earth. In order to teach men more fully this mystery, which was but foreshadowed in the Old Testament, God himself came down from angels unto men: "No man hath seen God at any time; the only begotten Son, who is in the bosom of the Father, he hath declared him" (John 1:18). Of Him, St. Paul writes, "For of him, and by him, and in him, are all things: to him be glory for ever" (Rom. 11:36).

These words signify both the Trinity of Persons and the unity of nature: for as this is one and the same in each of the Persons, so to each is equally owing supreme glory, as to one and the same God. Augustine, commenting on this testimony, writes that "the words of the Apostle, OF HIM, and BY HIM, and IN HIM," are not to be taken indiscriminately; OF HIM refers to the Father, BY HIM to the Son, IN HIM to the Holy Spirit." It is most fitting to attribute to the Father those works of divinity in which power (authority) excels, to the Son those in which wisdom excels, and to the Holy Spirit those in which love excels. Not that all perfections and external operations are not common to the Divine Persons; for "the operations of the Trinity are indivisible, even as the essence of the Trinity is indivisible" (Aquinas) because as the three Divine Persons "are inseparable, so do they act inseparably" (Augustine). But by a certain comparison, and a kind of affinity between the operations and the properties of the Persons, these operations are attributed or, as it is said, "appropriated" to, One Person rather than to others. "Just as we make use of the traces of similarity or likeness which we find in creatures for the manifestation of the Divine Persons, so do we use their essential attributes; and this manifestation of the Persons by their essential attributes is called appropriation" (Aquinas). In this manner the Father, who is "the principle of the whole Godhead" (Augustine), is also the efficient cause of all things, of the Incarnation of the Word, and the sanctification of souls; "of Him are all things," *of Him,* referring to the Father. But the Son, the Word, the image of God, is also the exemplar cause, whence all creatures borrow their form and beauty, their order and harmony. He is for us the way, the truth, and the life; the reconciler of man with God. "*By* Him are all things," *by Him* referring to the Son.

The Holy Spirit is the ultimate cause of all things, since, as the will and all other things finally rest in their end, so He the divine goodness and the mutual love of the Father and the Son *completes* and *perfects,* by His strong yet gentle power, the secret work of man's eternal salvation. "*In* Him are all things"—"Him" referring to the Holy Spirit (*Divinum Illud Munus,* by Pius XII).

From all that we have studied thus far it must be quite evident that opposition to Christ stems not so much from the bad faith of man alone, and his bad will, but from powers that are diabolical. Yet, withal, man is responsible, because of his freedom and God's grace, for his own works, despite the power of Satan: "I can do all things *in* him [the Holy Spirit] who strengthens me" (Phil. 4:13).

Despite all the opposition, one can gain and retain control of the situation because of faith born of God and nourished with His grace plus the dimension of the certitude of faith coming from the infallibility of the teaching Church, which shall occupy our attention at some great length.

CHAPTER 15

The Sheepfold I—Peter the Porter

When one hears the word *sheepfold*, one instinctively turns to the tenth chapter in John. One scarce can appreciate the delicate tones of the parable of the good shepherd and the sheepfold without a briefing on the sheep industry of Palestine. The Jewish people, as everyone knows, offered lambs in sacrifice at their important feasts, as public worship to God. Many families owned sheep. The sheep pastured or grazed on what was known as "the commons" at the outside of the villages and towns, on the mountainsides. Of a morning, some member of the family would lead his handful of sheep out to pasture. This, multiplied by many, many owners, resulted in a flock of sheep to be counted in the hundreds. Instead of each family remaining to tend its own sheep, the whole large flock was shepherded by one or more hireling shepherds (hired men). When night came, and with it the time to take the sheep home, the huge flock had to be separated so that each small bunch might return to its owner's barn.

You and I, who are not familiar with sheep, will wonder how they each ever got their own separated from the entire flock on the mountainside! It would seem that a whole night must be spent in separating one's own from the others. So it would seem to the uninitiated, but not to one familiar with sheep.

Each owner (or a representative) would appear at the pasture on the commons. Each owner would merely call, "Sheep, sheep, sheep." After a few calls each sheep would "recognize its own master's voice" and would scamper off in the direction of that voice. Yes, it was just that easy, for such is the loyalty of sheep. Soon the sheep would be at home locked behind the door in the sheepfold. No sooner said than done.

Memories of the above happenings, witnessed so very often by our dear Lord, surely must have given rise to the following parable found in John 10:1 ff:

1. Amen, amen, I say to you: He that entereth not by the door of the sheep [Greek reading] into the sheepfold, but climbeth up some other way, the same is a thief and a robber.

2. But he that entereth by the door is the shepherd of the sheep.

3. To him the porter openeth; and the sheep hear his voice: and he calleth his own sheep by name, and leadeth them out.

4. And when he hath let out his own sheep, he goeth before them: and the sheep follow him, because they know his voice.

5. But a stranger they follow not, but fly from him, because they know not the voice of strangers.

6. This proverb Jesus spoke to them. But they understood not what he spoke to them.

7. Jesus therefore said to them again: Amen, amen, I say to you, I am the door of the sheep.

8. All others, as many as have come, are thieves and robbers: and the sheep hear them not.

9. I am the door. By me, if any man enter in, he shall be saved: and he shall go in, and go out, and shall find pastures.

10. The thief cometh not, but for to steal, and to kill, and to destroy. I am come that they may have life and have it more abundantly.

11. I am the good shepherd. The good shepherd giveth his life for his sheep.

12. But the hireling, and he that is not the shepherd . . . leaves . . .

13. And the hireling flieth because he is a hireling and careth not for the sheep.

14. I am the good shepherd; and I know mine and mine know me.

15. As the Father knoweth me, and I know the Father; and I lay down my life for my sheep.

16. And other sheep I have, that are not of this fold: them also I must bring, and they shall hear my voice, and there shall be one fold and one shepherd. . . .

25. Jesus answered them: I speak to you, and you believe not. . . .

26. But you do not believe because you are not of my sheep.

27. My sheep hear my voice: and I know them and they follow me.

28. And I give them life everlasting; and they shall not perish forever, and no man shall pluck them out of my hand.

29. That which my Father hath given me is greater than all: and no one can snatch them out of the hand of my Father.

30. I and the Father are one. . . .

34. Jesus answered them: Is it not written in your law: I said you are gods?

35. . . . He called them gods to whose ears the word of God came and the Scriptures cannot be annulled [my Greek translation].

The above parable was delivered to the Apostles early in their "school days" with the dear Lord. The record states that the Apostles did not understand the parable as it was delivered unto them. However, the record fails to tell us if they understood after Jesus had given further explanation. Perhaps nowhere in all the messages of our Lord was He quite so subtle. But this much is true: the Apostles will not have failed to understand the proverb, after having received later on, the spirit of understanding, as we shall see, namely, on Pentecost Sunday.

The above parable presents a seeming contradiction upon first reading, but upon closer analysis it becomes clear from the Lord's own interpretation given to His words.

First of all, Jesus says in verse 2 "he that entereth by the door is the shepherd of the sheep." Then in verses 11 and 14, He says that He is the good shepherd. In verses 7 and 9 He says He is the door of the sheep. The question that is perplexing is this: If He is the "door," how can He at the same time be the shepherd that goes in and out of the door? Then in verse 3, He states that "the porter openeth the door to him."

What is the explanation? It is important to keep in mind, first of all, that Jesus identifies the "sheep" as men: "I am the door. By me, if any *man* enter in he shall be saved: and he shall go in and go out, and shall find pastures."

Next, in verses 11 and 14, Jesus tells us how He is the *good* shepherd: because "the *good* shepherd [One is good, and He is God: Matt. 19:17] giveth his life for his Sheep; and I know mine and mine know me." Continuing, He says in verse 15: "As the Father knoweth me and I know the Father; and I lay down my life for my sheep." This is to say that Jesus, the Son of God, and the Father share the same common divine life. So His sheep will also share and partake of that divine life. "As I live by the Father, so he that eateth me the same shall live by me" (John 6:58). In this wise is He directly the Good Shepherd, because He is not a hireling that cares not for the life of the sheep. Jesus does care, and for this He died, "that they may have divine life and have it more abundantly" (v. 10). That is, divine life shall increase as they grow in His holiness in becoming the whole man, the finished man. Man shall approximate more and more the likeness of God.

To remove the perplexity stated above about Jesus being "the door" and the *Good* Shepherd, we must return to the first part of the parable. At the very outset Jesus implied that the door of the sheep into the sheepfold was locked because the thieves and robbers enter not by the door, but climb up another way. Continuing, Jesus said, "But he that enters by the door is the shepherd of the sheep. To him the porter opens; and the sheep hear his voice: and he calleth his own sheep by name, and leadeth them out." The perplexity referred to above about Jesus being the door and at the same time the shepherd going in and out resolves itself if one keep in mind that Jesus speaks of two shepherds. The one is Himself, the *Good Shepherd,* and the other is simply a human shepherd. Jesus contrasts one with the other. There is no sin in Him.

Locked doors suggest keys. And when one thinks of keys, one thinks of the porter who carries the keys.

It is now time to ask the question: Who has the keys? The porter, of course. And who is the porter? Turning to Matthew, I read that to Simon, son of Jonas, He said, ". . . Peter, to thee I will give the keys of the kingdom of heaven" (16:16 ff.). Note the future tense of the promise!

Here we have it. Peter will have the keys. Peter is the porter. Peter the porter will unlock the door, Christ. Peter will unlock the door of the sheep into the sheepfold. Christ is the door. Peter is to be the porter who is to be given the keys by Christ. Peter must be that other shepherd Jesus referred to.

The seeming contradiction now disappears because Jesus is speaking of the shepherd in two distinct senses—because there are to be two shepherds. Jesus says so. In verses 11 and 14 He calls Himself the "good" shepherd who pays the price for salvation. In that sense He is also the door. However, in verses 2 and 3 Jesus speaks not of the "good" shepherd but simply of the "shepherd." "But he that entereth by the door is the shepherd of the sheep. To him the good shepherd, the porter opens; and the sheep hears his voice: and he calls his own sheep by name, and leads them out. And when he has let out his own sheep, he goes before them [prevening grace]: and the sheep follow him, because they know his voice (2-4). "I am the door. By me, if any man enter in, he shall be saved and he shall go in, and go out, and shall find pastures" (9). Peter is that shepherd who is to be the Vicar of the Good Shepherd. Since Peter, the "shepherd," is to go in and out of that door, that means he too must believe as all others.

This same Jesus who said, "I am the door" is also the one who said, "I am the way, and the truth, and the life" (John 14:6). He it was who also said, "Unless one [tis] is born again of water and the Holy Spirit he cannot *enter* the kingdom of God," that is, the sheepfold (John 3:5). Through faith, Baptism of water, and the Holy Spirit, a man enters through Christ the door.

It is, therefore, Peter the porter who has the keys to unlock the door, Christ, to His truth and divine life as the Way to eternal life. Peter the porter is Christ's other self. He is Christ's other voice. Peter is Christ's Vicar. Peter is the vicarious voice of Christ calling the sheep and leading them to and fro to pasture. Peter feeds the truth. Peter feeds the divine life in the seven sacraments. Peter guides, by his laws, the sheep: "I will give to you the keys of the kingdom of heaven [my sheep-fold] that whatsoever you shall bind upon earth [among men] it shall be bound also in heaven; and whatsoever you shall loose upon earth it shall also be loosed in heaven [confirmed in heaven, that is]."

Peter opens the door, Christ, to those who have the Spirit of Christ. The Father shepherds each soul, the Son shepherds each soul, and the Holy Spirit shepherds each soul, because all works are common to the three Divine Persons. Not only is each soul or person shepherded individually, but the entire sheepfold corporately is also shepherded as one whole. "They who are baptized in Christ have put on Christ" (Gal. 3:27). They have the Spirit of Christ in them: the Spirit that furnishes the life from the Father and the Son for the individual as well as for the whole religion-family-man; the sheepfold: His assembly.

Christ brings this out so subtly that it is not quickly discernible from the present parable. Note these words: "And I give them life everlasting [divine life, that is]; and they shall not perish forever, and no man shall pluck them out of my hand. That which my Father hath given me is greater than all: and no one can snatch them out of the hand of my Father. I and the Father are one" (28-30).

Here Jesus is telling us that those who accept and retain the gift of the Holy Spirit, "who is greater than all" which He and the Father give, shall not perish forever. He also states that no one will pluck them out of "my hand," nor "snatch them out of the hand of my Father." What does the word *hand* mean? It refers, even among men, to a "helping hand," a hired hand as we say. Here the hand is the Holy Spirit. He is the hand of the Father and the Son. Jesus says so: "And I will ask the Father, and he shall give you *another* helping hand [Paraclete], that he may abide with you forever. . . . If anyone love me, he will *keep* my word, and my Father will love him, and we will come to him, and will make our abode with him" in the indwelling of the Holy Spirit." Continuing, Jesus says, "These things have I spoken to you, abiding with you. But the Paraclete, the Holy Spirit, whom the Father will send in my name, he will teach you all things, and bring all things to your mind whatsoever I shall have said to you" (John 14:16-26).

Note well, in chapter 10, where John gives us the parable of the sheepfold and the door, Jesus keeps the wraps, so to speak on the Holy Spirit, the third Person, but, four chapters later, John begins to unveil the Holy Spirit to them and through them to us.

When Jesus says "that which the Father has given to me is greater than all' (v. 29), He, Jesus, is referring veiledly to the Holy Spirit. Why is the Holy Spirit greater than all? Because He operates Operation Understanding; He operates sanctification, etc., etc.

When Jesus says, "No man shall pluck them out of my hand," He means just that. But when He says, "And no one can *snatch* them out of the hand of my Father," He is referring to Serpent, who *snatched* Parent and his family Man out of the hand of the Father. *Snatch* is the telltale word. It connotes stealth—serpent-like. "Out of my Father's hand" reminds one of the Holy Spirit, the Spirit of Holiness, from whom Parent and the whole religion family was "seduced," by original sin.

It must be kept in mind that the battle is on—the battle of the enmity between Serpent and the woman, between her Family and Serpent's family (Gen. 3:15), as we studied it in the great prohecy.

An observation worthy of mention is this: Jesus seldom mentions the devil by name—never more than He is constrained to. That thoughts of the Evil One were in Jesus' mind throughout this part of the gospel is evidenced in John's fourteenth chapter referred to above: "And now I have told you before it come to pass, that, when it shall come to pass, you may *believe*. I will not now speak many things to you. For *the prince of this world cometh, and in me hath not anything*" (John 14:29-30). Why is Jesus not going to speak much? Because Satan cannot read one's mind unless he first opens it up by speaking. Or unless God should strike him mute. Now you see why the Blessed Mother observed the virtue of silence. And why St. James could say, "He that offends not with the tongue is a perfect man."

"The prince of this world," of course, is the devil. He has "nothing in Jesus," meaning Satan does not yet know for sure that Jesus, the Son of the Man, is also the Son of God— Satan's mortal enemy, "the seed of the woman."

St. Irenaeus testified that in apostolic times "the hand" or the "arm" of God referred to God the Son and the Holy Spirit. Here, the word *hand* is used because it is not here a symbol of creation but a symbol of friendship: "I have called you friends" (John 15:15). The hand of fellowship. (Cf. Gal. 2:9; Phil. 3:10; I John 1:36.)

Note, too, in the text above: "My Father shall give you *another* Paraclete" (14:16). This is to say, without actually saying it, that Jesus is a *helper* too. *Paraclete* means "helper" in the sense of "advocate." A lawyer is an advocate, a helper (hired hand), for his client in matters that pertain to the mind and understanding for those who are naturally deficient. And who will say that poor mankind is not deficient in the wake of Satan's prevarications!

"The sheep shall hear his Voice—and he goeth before them, and they follow him because they know his voice." Whose voice? The voice of the Spirit as Peter leads the sheep to Christ.

Peter's voice is Christ's voice. Peter the porter shall call the sheep. The Holy Spirit shall illuminate that "calling" (Eph. 4:1), and "they shall hear my voice [Peter] and they shall follow me." Jesus does not say, "They shall hear my voice and follow Peter." No; but, "They shall hear my voice and follow *me*." They shall hear the "voice" of my shepherd and they shall follow me, the good shepherd. This is promised infallibility, but not impeccability.

Vv. 14-15: "I know mine and mine know me—just as I know the Father, and the Father knows me—because I and the Father are one." So shall my sheep be one religion-family—Christ. This is the sheepfold; the kingdom of my love; the kingdom of God; the family of the "woman."

If this unanimity of voice between Christ and Peter seems difficult to grasp, let us appeal to other examples:

"God, who at sundry times and in divers manners spoke in times past to the fathers by the voice of the prophets, last of all in these times hath spoken to us by his Son" (Heb. 1:1). Now, the "Son of [the] Man" is not a human person. Nevertheless, God the Father spoke through God the Son, using the physical voice of the Son of the Man's human nature.

God also spoke, through the assumed voice of the angel Gabriel, to Mary. God spoke through the voice of John the Baptist.

When John said, "I am the voice of one crying in the wilderness," he was not referring to his own voice box. But he was revealing the fact that he, John, who also "was sent," was only the vicarious voice of *One,* Yahweh, "sent from God" (John 1:6, 23). The term "of One" refers not to one John but to Him who was sent, namely, the Messiah, or Yahweh, as the last text indicates. Messiah means the one who was *sent* by the Father.

"But all things whatsoever John said of this man were true" (John 10:42). They were not true because John said them—"I receive not testimony from man" (John 5:34)—but because they were true, John had to say them, being the voice of God operating under the influence of the Holy Spirit. "But I receive not testimony from man, but I say these things that you may be saved" (John 5:34). "John was a burning and shining light, and for a time you followed John" (John 5:35). What I, Jesus, wanted, was for you to listen to my vicarious voice in John, and follow, not John but me. This you did not do. And now, "for whom he [the Father] hath sent, him you believe not," namely, Christ. (John 5:38 ff.) "Your faith must stand not on the wisdom of the world, but on the power of God" (I Cor. 2:5). My sheep, therefore, will hear my voice vested conjunctively in Peter the porter, and conjunctively, they shall follow me, together with Peter. For so soon as they hear me speaking through Peter and begin to believe me, then is it that the Holy Spirit is giving them understanding. "Unless you believe you will not understand."

Again, who is "my voice"? Scriptural history answers that question in Acts 15:7.

When, therefore, there was doubt, argument, and contention about a matter of faith or discipline among the official teachers, Paul, who had the faith, buried his self-pride, he the learned one, to go to the "unlettered" Peter the porter, to obtain the final answer of truth (cf. Acts 19:1 ff.).

CHAPTER 16

The Sheepfold II—Peter the Porter

It is fascinating how our Lord bends words to His revelations. Note, He does not say, "They shall hear my voice and they shall follow my voice," as sentences ordinarily run. No; He says, "They shall heed [hear] the voice of my porter, Peter, and they shall follow me"—the way, the truth, and the life.

This is to say: "You will be infallibly safe in following the *voice* of Peter; but it is not to say that he, Peter, will be always *impeccable.* Peter will have to merit heaven by fighting the devil the same as all men [Luke 22:32]. You are safe in following Peter's voice—because his voice is my voice—he is my Vicar. You are safe in believing it is my voice only when you hear him propose my revelations for belief. Believe those truths, and then follow, not Peter but me together with Peter. Peter must believe what He voices the same as all others before him believed and taught." Now we understand why Jesus says, "I am the good shepherd" (John 10:11, 14) and why He refers to a second "shepherd" whom He does not qualify as good or not good (John 10:2, 16).

Now we know what Jesus meant when He said, "He that heareth you heareth me; and he that despiseth you despiseth me; and . . . him that sent me" (Luke 10:16; see also Matt. 28:18-20; Mark 16:15-16).

At long last Jesus has explained for us the enigmatic word He spoke to Nicodemus anent "his voice":

"Wonder not that I said to thee, Ye must be born again. The Spirit [of Christ] breatheth where he will, and thou hearest his *voice,* but thou knowest not whence he originates, and whether he goeth: so it is with everyone that is born of the Spirit. Nicodemus answered, and said to him: How can these things be done? Jesus answered: Art thou a master [teacher] in Israel, and knowest not these things? . . . *We* testify . . . and you receive not *our* testimony" (you do not have the Holy Spirit) John 3:7-12.) Nicodemus, who was a "master," should have known that all learners are not to question their own master's voice but rather to heed it if they wish to learn.

We testify through our voice, Peter the porter, the shepherd. Peter and I are one voice, one shepherd, one head. He is the porter because he does the earthly menial chores like a servant-porter. That makes Peter my Vicar on earth. He is the servant of the servants of the Lord, who is ascended into heaven (John 3:13).

Parent's responsibility in Eden was bound up with *impeccability* (sinlessness). Peter the porter's responsibility is bound up, *not* with *impeccability* but with *infallibility*. The gates of hell (Serpent) shall not *prevail* against *my* religion-family (the Church.) I will give to you, Peter, the keys of the religion-family, the kingdom of heaven. Whatsoever you shall bind upon earth, as my porter, the same shall be bound also in heaven. These keys shall unlock "the door" to the drink of the Spirit in the seven sacraments; and to the food of the "pastures": revealed truth, which is by faith, and you shall rule over all with the binding and loosing force of law. I will be with you on earth, from my throne in heaven. You will be my vicarious authority on earth. I will be the real head in heaven. We shall be as one in authority; visible, as such, only to the eyes of faith.

Peter will preach the truth, but men must pray for the light of the Holy Spirit to be enabled to accept that truth. "If you believe not you will not understand." "You have not because you ask not."

Jesus said, "Amen, amen, I say to thee, unless one is born

from above he cannot see the kingdom of God" (John 3:3). This "rebirth" is the invisible Baptism. The illumination of the Holy Spirit calls, urges, draws one to want to know more about Christ, God, and to love Him more. Finally, if such a one does not resist that grace, that "seed" (see Matt. 13:3 ff.), he will ask Peter the porter to unlock the "door," for "Amen, amen, I say to you unless one is reborn of water and the Holy Spirit he *cannot enter* the sheepfold." Did not Jesus also say, "They all shall be taught of God" (John 3:45)? He said too, "Faith cometh by hearing, and hearing by the word of God" (Rom. 10:17). As soon as one believes and is baptized with water and the Holy Spirit, that one becomes a member of the sheepfold. Christ, in the Holy Spirit, shepherds the sheep of the flock individually as well as collectively with the "abundant life" (John 10:10) of His grace administered through the other sacraments. The Holy Spirit, the Spirit of Christ, from the Father and the Son, shepherds the flock.

V. 3: To Him, the Holy Spirit, Peter the porter opens the flood gates of Christ's grace, which grace operates by the Holy Spirit coporately in His body, the Church. Peter the porter opens the door when he selects ministers who become the instruments in administering the sacraments, while the Holy Spirit dispenses the grace of each of the sacraments into the soul of the person receiving the sacraments. Those "other sheep" outside the fold are being cheated. They want for His "voice."

V. 3: The sheep hear Peter's voice. Loyal Christians always have heard His voice, according to history, unless, no longer believing because of private judgment, they put off Christ, and returned to that brotherhood of man under the empire of Satan (II Pet. 2:14-22).

V. 3: "And Peter calleth his own sheep by *name,* and he leads them out, etc., etc." This, Scriptural history verifies

(Eph. 4:11). Isaias had said, "Your Maker is your husband, the Lord of hosts is his name" (Isa. 54:5).

No, the sacraments are not superstitious practices, as some without faith maintain. They are but simple signs instituted by Christ, which, if placed as He prescribed, will infallibly produce their effects. For example, water is a sign of washing on the natural level. Hence on the supernatural level it is the sign of cleansing which Christ so ordained. The sacraments, therefore, are His ordinances. When God the Father made Christ the head of the new family, He also sent the Holy Spirit to be the soul of that family, uniting all lambs and sheep into one "flock" or "body." Baptism does several things. It cleanses from sin. It makes the man "whole" with God's abiding presence. It makes one a member of the Church. Just as we say the soul of man is whole and entire in his whole body, and whole and entire in each part of his body, so also is the Holy Spirit of Christ whole and entire in the whole body or assembly, and He is whole and entire in each member of Christ's new body. The Holy Spirit, therefore, being the "Maker" of those whom He would make, makes not only "the member in particular," His spouse; He makes the entire body, as a whole, His spouse, and He is "the husband." The corporate body, the Church, is His bride. He is preparing this bride, now on earth, for the wedding in heaven. Such is love. Thus it is that we say Mother Church. At the end of time it will be the Church triumphant in victory.

Accordingly, as our whole body is called human in the natural order, and each member is named heart, lungs, spleen, etc., so is it with Christ's new supernatural body. The whole body with all the members "together" is named "Christ" (I Cor. 12:12 ff.).

This is not all. The Shepherd "calls them individually by names." The Shepherd, the Holy Spirit—the Spirit of Christ, operating as one head, with Peter the shepherd—singles out certain sheep and "calls them by name." Some He calls bishops, pastors; some He calls evangelists; others, apostles, disciples, presbyters or priests, deacons, teachers, and so on. (Eph. 4:11; I Pet. 4:7-11.) But to each of these He says, "Let no one take unto himself this office unless he is called . . . unless he is sent," officially, by Peter the Vicar. Hence, when Paul says, "The Holy Spirit has placed you bishops to rule the church of God" (Acts 20:28), he includes Peter in that shepherding of the "sheep" because Peter, after the Apostles, gave them the name of bishop for the office Christ instituted (Matt. 18:18). Both are one shepherd. Christ, through the Holy Spirit, and Peter, his mouthpiece, or voice, are the one Shepherd and the bishops are collegialites with Peter. Christ and Peter are one head. The Holy Spirit is the one life of the fold. The bishops appointed by Peter are one with him. Without Peter they are nil, even *collegialiter,* according to Vatican II, because "all authority is from God" and Peter is His Vicar.

Such it has been from the beginning of the Church, and such it ever shall be. Peter rules and teaches. The Holy Spirit inspires, teaches and sanctifies. Today, again, as in the past, Satan is getting his oar in; stirring things up; muddying the waters on which the barque of Peter sails. The scum is bound to come to the top, but the waters of hell shall not prevail.

At this juncture let us return to the parable of the good shepherd and take up those other words of our dear Lord which till now have gone unrecognized. Continuing, Jesus said, "And other sheep I have that are not of this fold: them too I must bring, and they shall hear my voice, and there shall be one fold and one shepherd. . . . My sheep hear my voice . . . and they follow me" (John 10:16, 27).

Who are "the other sheep"? The other sheep are those who, although having a good will, have not heard and learned as yet of His "voice." Not having learned, *supernaturally,* that Peter is the Master's voice, they naturally will not have asked Peter to unlock the "door" to the sheepfold, and of course will not have entered *by* the door of the sheep into the sheepfold: the brotherhood of Christ. Listen to Paul:

"They that are according to the flesh [i.e., on the natural level] mind the things of the flesh [i.e., human nature with its reason alone]. But they that are according to the Spirit [i.e., the supernatural level with the eye of faith] mind the things of the Holy Spirit [again of the supernatural]. If anyone does not have the Spirit of Christ, he does not belong to Christ" (Rom. 8:9). "For, whoever are led by the Spirit of God, they are the sons of God—who have received the spirit of adoption whereby we cry, Abba, meaning Father. For the Spirit giveth testimony to our spirit that we are the sons of God [that is, the informed voice of conscience]. And if sons, heirs also; heirs indeed of God, and joint heirs with Christ: yet so if we suffer with him, that we may be also glorified with him" (Rom. 8:5-17).

Behold, the brotherhood of Christ! After sacramental Baptism of water we are no longer heirs of fallen Adam but joint heirs with Christ. "And if we suffer, we shall also reign with him. If we deny him, he will deny us. If we believe not, he continueth faithful, for he cannot deny himself." (II Tim. 2:12-13.) This is to be expected, because, "all who will live godly in Christ Jesus shall suffer persecution" (II Tim. 3:12) as Serpent lies in wait to polish off their heels.

Truthfully, therefore, can it be said of Peter, who is the voice of Christ: Your hands are the hands of the fisherman, but your voice is the voice of Christ. Peter, therefore, cannot err, if ever and whenever he bespeaks solemnly and officially (which may be once or twice in a century) the revelations of Christ. For it is Christ who speaks in and through Peter. And Christ can say honestly to all: "He that will not hear my voice vested in Peter, let him be accursed" (Mark 16:16);

"let him be to thee as the heathen and the publican"—social outcasts, offal (Mark 19:15). After Jesus' Ascension into heaven Peter's voice becomes Christ's voice: and Christ's inaudible voice becomes Peter's audible voice. Their voice is as one. But only the ears of faith are able to hear that voice.

Again, who are the "other sheep"? The other sheep are those who have received the sacramental Baptism of water but have not learned and known that they are under obligation to heed Peter's voice. This, because of their upbringing, and through no fault of their own. There is only one laver of regeneration (Eph. 5:26). And those who have received this "bath" automatically become members of His sheepfold, because He has only *one* sheepfold. Since Jesus said, "Amen, amen, I say to thee unless one is born again of water and the Holy Spirit, he *cannot enter* the [sheepfold of] the kingdom of heaven," surely the opposite must be true. Those who are born again of water and the Holy Spirit must enter it. But if they are not educated to it, how will they know how to follow Peter in and out, to and from, pasture!

Further be it asked, who are the "other sheep"? The other sheep are they who have not learned of the Baptism of water, but who have, by the grace of God, received that invisible sacrament of Baptism (as St. Augustine called it) which is a perfect act of love for God. There can be, of course, no love for God unless first there has been the minimum of faith. Paul says, "But without faith it is impossible to please God. For he that cometh to God must first believe that He is, and is a rewarder to them that seek him" (Heb. 11:6). And Jesus said, "Unless one is born from above [invisible Baptism] he cannot *see* the kingdom of God." The urge for God, He has put in all men at the time of birth: "He enlightens every man that comes into the world" John 1:10).

Is there any hope for the above classes, "the other sheep"?

If, with a good conscience, and not malice, they are where they are, there is hope. Mark was Peter's secretary, and this is what he wrote: "John said: 'Master, we saw one casting out devils in thy name, who followeth not us, and we forbade him.' But Jesus said, 'Do not forbid him. For there is no man that doth a miracle in my name, and can soon speak ill of me. For *he that is not against you, is for you.*'" (Mark 9:37-39.)

Paul had something similar to say in behalf of those who *received* the preaching of Christ: Some are preaching Christ out of brotherly love for me who am appointed to preach the gospel. But others are preaching the Christ, not sincerely, but out of rivalry, or envy, as if to make my imprisonment affliction harder to bear. What's the difference, whether it be from true motives or false motives, just so that Christ be preached! For in this I rejoice, and shall continue to rejoice, for in this I know that through your prayers and the grace of the Spirit of the Lord Jesus Christ this shall turn out to my salvation. (Phil. 1:13-20.)

Referring to the words from Mark above, some will say, "Strange words, these!" At first blush they do appear to be strange words. But when one recalls the justice of God, as well as His mercy, they do not appear so strange. For God will not condemn anyone through no fault of his own. And surely the "other sheep" who through no fault of their own have failed to find their way, together with Peter the porter, through the door of the sheep into the sheepfold shall not be condemned. Such are, in one sense of the word, still on the outside of the sheepfold, being nourished by "the crumbs that fall from the table of their masters" (Matt. 15:27; Mark 7:28; Luke 16:21). As was stated in a preceding chapter, the words of the preacher do not effect the conversion as does the grace of God.

The few divine truths which they have access to, and by

which they live in His name, have come from Christ and Peter through Peter's having preserved incorrupted God's Sacred Scriptures. They are on the outside getting their light and warmth from what escapes through the window. They are on the outside looking in.

Inversely, such might also be said to be in the state of spiritual gestation, or in the elementary grades of His religion. Factually and physically and actually they do not as yet belong to the sheepfold, because they are not recognizing Peter the porter in a direct and forthright way. But since they are acting in Jesus' name, as they understand it, and not Satan's, to their best ability, they are at the same time implicitly recognizing Peter, because Peter and Jesus are as one head to the whole world. Such cannot be said to be "outside" the sheepfold entirely, in another sense of the word (*extra*), for the simple reason they are still not beyond the realms of that sheepfold's influence: but within the realms of its influence, even though, in perfectly good faith, they do not recognize it. They belong to the fold by way of good faith, and love or implicit desire. And no doubt there are many saints among them.

The preceding paragraph explains the meaning of the following words that so often give rise to objection: "Outside the Church there is no salvation." That text was originally done in Latin. The word for "outside" (*extra*) means "beyond the realm of influence." For those beyond the realms of the Church's influence, there is no salvation. This is true because our Lord said, "A city seated on a mountain top cannot be hid" (Matt. 5:14). "Their voice has gone forth into all the earth—to the ends of the world" (Rom. 10:18). This is to say that all can be influenced if they will to be. And anyone who gets to heaven owes it to that influence, whether he knew it or not when on earth.

The foregoing text, therefore, is not to say that all who

are not tucked within the confines of Peter the porter's fold shall be lost forever if it is through no fault of their own. But it is to say that everyone who shall get to heaven must possess at least a minimum of what Christ offers through His Church: "For he that cometh to God must believe that He is, and is a rewarder to them that seek him" (Heb. 11:6). Such a minimum, anyone, no matter who or where, can have. Such is God's infinite mercy.

This in turn is not to say that one can be satisfied with the minimum. Every man must be informed by a true conscience. This conscience he must form by prayer and by following the light God gives him. He must be taught. "Faith cometh by hearing," not by reading (Rom. 10:17).

As to the state of those not in the Church, God will be their judge. When a nasty situation was presented to Jesus, He said, "With man this is impossible, but with God all things are possible" (Matt. 19:26).

I have come across many, many of them, when they came to be taught and to be admitted into the sheepfold. They did not have to change their lives. They merely graduated to better and greater and fuller pastures. Then they no longer had to feed on the "crumbs." They came on the table and partook of all the dear Lord left for all those who shall hear His voice and come into His sheepfold for "the abundant life." In every instance their only regret was that they had not done it sooner! They fulfilled Paul's other words: "He that believeth shall not be disappointed" (Rom. 10:11).

It is safe to say, therefore, that those who are active members shall receive the severest judgment. Did not Jesus say that "to whom much is given much shall be required, but to him who has received but little, little shall be expected" (Luke 12:48)?

BRIGHT: There is a lot of noise in the media these days

about "identifying with the poor." Is there anything new
about that?

FATHER: The terminology is new, and also the activities of
late are new. Perhaps the counrty is half a century behind
the times, if not more so. We used to say, "Put yourself
in the other fellow's boots." It was not such high-toned
English. But your own expression being more sophisticated, the sophisticates are becoming alerted.

BRIGHT: What does the Bible have to say about it?

FATHER: Plenty. But strange as it may seem, hardly any
one paid any attention to it until Pope John, was it, caused
it to catch fire. Please read this long quote from Matthew
25:31-46.

BRIGHT: OK.

"But when the Son of [the] Man shall come in his
majesty, and all the angels with him, then he will sit on
the throne of his glory; and before him will be gathered
all the nations, and he will separate them one from
another, as the shepherd separates the sheep from the
goats; and he will set the sheep on his right hand, but
the goats on the left. Then the king will say to those on
his right hand, 'Come, blessed of my Father, take possession of the kingdom prepared for you from the foundation
of the world; for I was hungry and you gave me to eat;
I was thirsty and you gave me to drink; I was a stranger
and you took me in, naked and you covered me; sick
and you visited me. . . . Then the just will answer him,
saying, 'Lord, when did we see thee hungry, and feed
thee; or thirsty, and give thee drink? And when did we
see thee a stranger, and take thee in; or naked, and
clothe thee? Or when did we see thee sick, or in prison,
and come to thee?' And answering the king will say to

them, 'Amen I say to you, as long as you did it for one of these, the least of my brethren, you did it for me.' Then he will say to those on his left hand, 'Depart from me, accursed ones, into the everlasting fire which was prepared for the devil and his angels. For I was hungry, and you did not give me to eat; I was thirsty and you gave me no drink; I was a stranger and you did not take me in: naked, and you did not clothe me; sick, and in prison, and you did not visit me.' Then they also will answer and say, 'Lord, when did we see thee hungry, or thirsty, or a stranger, or naked, or sick, or in prison, and did not minister to thee?' Then he will answer them, saying, 'Amen I say to you, as long as you did not do it for one of these least ones, you did not do it for me.' And these will go into everlasting punishment, but the just into everlasting life."

There is no doubt about those last words getting one involved!

FATHER: Yes, and while identifying with all those mentioned by our Lord we are doing His thing while at the same time we are doing our own thing. If we know anything from the Bible we should know that God has always had a heart of compassion, which the very word *mercy* means. And of His mercy, the Bible says it is above His justice.

BRIGHT: It would appear men in the past have strayed rather far from the rules of God for the game of life and on how to get to heaven.

FATHER: You can say that again and again.

BRIGHT: There's an old saying that has it, "If you wish to make an enemy, then you should be sure to befriend someone in need."

FATHER: What you say is largely true because envy is afforded a fine opportunity for gaining entrance. I would suggest you contribute to the local church's charity fund and remain anonymous, with no chance for envy to enter and at the same time for not letting your left hand know what your right hand does. Do not these words of our Lord seem to anticipate the very problem you alluded to?

When St. Paul wrote, "For by grace you have been saved through faith; and that not from yourselves, for it is the gift of God; not as the outcome of words, lest anyone may boast, for his workmanship we are, created in Christ Jesus in good works," he described the name of the game of life, which is Going Her Way (Eph. 2:10).

The above texts are beautifully captured in the following poem by Father Tabb:

> My life is but a weaving
> Between my God and me,
> I may but choose the colors
> He worketh skillfully.
> Full oft He chooses sorrow
> And I in foolish pride
> Forget He sees the upper
> and I the under-side.

This is to say that at the beginning of the game of life, man's soul is akin to a piece of canvas or bare tapestry stretched across the loom of our mortal body.

Into this canvas the Creator expects the very likeness of Christ to be woven with His grace, "lest any man boast."

Under and up and through this canvas or tapestry, back and forth, day after day, the silken threads furnished by one or other of the seven sacraments are to be used.

With the cooperation of one's own good intentions, the fingers of the Holy Spirit and His spouse, Mary, together with the infused virtues of faith, hope, and charity and prudence, justice, temperance, and fortitude, together with all their son and daughter virtues, become the shuttles that weave His very likeness into the canvas of the soul. At the moment of death, God the Father first removes the tapestry from the loom for the final inspection which the Church calls the particular judgment. According to the measure of Christ's likeness, then formed in us, shall our reward be. This is done by going Her way, *which is His way*.

In conclusion, may it be stated that when St. Paul says the just man lives by faith, Paul is giving expression to every nuance of meaning that might be attached to the word *faith*. We have faith as a faculty created within the mind whereby we are enabled to see and understand God's revelations whether proposed in Scripture or in tradition or both, as proposed by the teaching Church. Then we have faith as an act which holds us in communication with God and so pleases him.

In other words, we must live and act and perform all of our duties in keeping with the principles of faith. To do so makes every action a work of faith and worthy of heavenly reward.

This faith reaches a great solace by keeping ever before us the Blessed Mother, who is Mother of the Church as well as the model for all Christians, She of whom Luke makes St. Elizabeth praise in the following words: "Blessed is she who has believed, because the things promised her by the Lord shall be accomplished" (Luke 1:45).

We can rest assured that our names in some way were enmeshed in the things that were promised Her, and with our good will they shall be accomplished.